Freely and Lightly blends a palette of depth, beauty, simplicity, real life, and rich truths to create an artful and compelling invitation to truly rest and enjoy refreshment for your soul.
—**Marilyn Vancil,** author of *Self to Lose, Self to Find: Using the Enneagram to Uncover Your True, God-Gifted Self*

We don't deserve *Freely and Lightly*, but we so desperately need this quiet masterpiece. In a time when life can be loud and abrasive, I'm so very grateful for Emily's gentle, lovely, and profound words.
—**Knox McCoy,** author of *All Things Reconsidered*

I wholeheartedly believe this: The more you believe God, the more confident you will become. Emily's relatable words and gentle encouragement to let go of self-reliance and to trust who God is and who he made us to be is exactly what women of all ages need to hear.
—**Alli Worthington,** author of *Standing Strong*, business coach, and cofounder of Called Creatives

In a culture conditioned to turn toward the loudest voice in the room, Emily Lex shows us the spiritual heft of a gentle soul. *Freely and Lightly* is an invitation to lay down our burdens, trading the trendy, self-comfort sort of rest for a deep gulp of living water. This book is fresh air and freedom.
—**Shannan Martin,** author of *The Ministry of Ordinary Places* and *Falling Free*

When I celebrated a huge milestone in my life several years ago, Emily Lex sent me a small watercolor of flowers she painted to say congratulations. Every time I look at that small framed painting on my desk, I feel seen and loved. Now we all get an entire book of paintings from Emily! I hope this book will do for you what that painting did for me. With simple beauty and deep faith, *Freely and Lightly* is the book we need when we feel overwhelmed, overlooked, and undone. I'm so grateful to Emily for this kind work of art.
—**Emily P. Freeman,** *Wall Street Journal* bestselling author of *The Next Right Thing*

This is my new favorite book to gift! Emily's watercolor art and hopeful insights offer grace and peace to all who read *Freely and Lightly*. You are going to love this little book.

—**Jessica N. Turner,** bestselling author of *The Fringe Hours* and *Stretched Too Thin*

Freely and Lightly is the friend who understands your weary soul, holds your hand, and walks you back toward the truth that brings true rest. Through vulnerable storytelling and exquisite artistry, Emily invites us to remember what it feels like to twirl—to be who we already are and to know the delight of our Father. Join me in reading and gifting this book again and again.

—**Nicole Zasowski,** marriage and family therapist and author of *From Lost to Found*

This book is sheer truth, goodness, and beauty—the hallmark trifecta of great art. The words and watercolors Emily has graced us with in these pages call to mind a deeper, more necessary truth than we normally see in the cacophony of life—that Christ reveals himself in the daily delights.

—**Tsh Oxenreider,** author of *Shadow & Light*, *At Home in the World*, and *Notes from a Blue Bike*

Cozy up in your favorite chair. Emily's winsome storytelling will draw you in, and her grace-filled insights and delightful artistry will cause you to linger long in these pages. You'll be glad you did.

—**Ruth Chou Simons,** *Wall Street Journal* bestselling author of *Beholding and Becoming* and *GraceLaced*, artist, and founder of gracelaced.com

As I read Emily's relatable, kind words, the tension in my shoulders relaxed, and I felt greater permission to be myself. *Freely and Lightly* is aptly named, offering a buoy for the tired soul.

—**Kendra Adachi,** *New York Times* bestselling author of *The Lazy Genius Way* and host of *The Lazy Genius* podcast

Emily has been bringing beauty into my life for many years now through both her art and her words. She has a unique way of pointing me back to Jesus over and over again in a style that leaves me feeling refreshed. *Freely and Lightly* is exactly what the world needs right now to help us fight the discouragement and disillusionment all around us. I know you will turn each page and feel your soul growing lighter and your faith becoming stronger.

—**Melanie Shankle,** *New York Times* bestselling author and speaker

As you read this book, you will feel your friend Emily's invitation to rest in all that Jesus has to offer. Her words are soothing, her stories are inviting, and her illustrations are beautiful. Grab a blanket, a cup of coffee, and this book, and prepare to be encouraged!

—**Jamie Ivey,** bestselling author and podcast host

freely

AND

lightly

EMILY LEX

HARVEST HOUSE PUBLISHERS
EUGENE, OREGON

Published in association with Illuminate Literary Agency

Cover and interior design by Connie Gabbert

Freely and Lightly
Text and artwork copyright © 2021 by Emily Lex
Published by Harvest House Publishers
Eugene, Oregon 97408
www.harvesthousepublishers.com

ISBN 978-0-7369-8037-1 (hardcover)
ISBN 978-0-7369-8038-8 (eBook)

Library of Congress Cataloging-in-Publication Data Record is available at https://lccn.loc.gov/2020025791.

Printed in China

20 21 22 23 24 25 26 27 28 29 / RDS – CG / 10 9 8 7 6 5 4 3 2 1

For the one who is tired and weary.

He really will make good on his promise.

CONTENTS

Are you tired?
Worn out? Burned out on religion?
Come to me.
Get away with me and you'll
recover your life.
I'll show you how to take a real rest.

Walk with me and work with me —
watch how I do it.
Learn the unforced rhythms of grace.
I won't lay anything heavy
or ill-fitting on you.
Keep company with me and you'll learn
to live freely and lightly.

MATTHEW 11:28-30 MSG

t-shirt

INTRODUCTION

THE FINE LINE

I have a T-shirt, and across the front in white block lettering, it reads #TIRED. It is supposed to be a cheeky tee you wear on lazy weekends or with pajama pants to bed or something an adorably overprimped Instagram influencer would put on for a perfectly styled selfie as she hugs a cup of coffee on a Monday morning. I bought it because at that time, I was literally #tired. My iron levels were dangerously low: If I didn't stop and get intravenous drips of liquid iron, I ran the risk of passing out while doing dishes.

Our bodies are magnificently perceptive and often the first to inform us that something's off. Mine was throwing flags and waving its arms and yelling at me, *Emily, this isn't working! You must slow down and pay attention.* My actions, my pace, my lifestyle, and my way of being were leading me in the wrong direction. My body crashing was the messenger of a much deeper truth I had known but not yet acknowledged: My soul had grown weary, and the things I was throwing at it to try to find satisfaction were not making it better. Something needed to change.

I'm beginning to believe that most people come to this turning point; it just happens at different times and seasons and for different reasons. Burdens are not spread around equally, just as our ability to adapt and deal is not equal. But I wonder if all of us eventually look at our lives and quietly ask, *Is this it? Is this all there is?* It sounds ungrateful, so most of us would never admit the dissatisfaction aloud, but it's there nevertheless.

This life that I've made for myself is not quite as I thought it would be.

This job is not as fulfilling as I dreamed.

My marriage is not making me happy.

I have a closet full of clothes with nothing to wear.

I didn't know parenthood was this hard.

The kids have grown up, and I'm not sure what to do with myself.

I'm dizzy, but if I stop for a second, the spinning plates will all come crashing down.

The problem is that none of these things were made for true, long-term satisfaction. No title, spouse, accomplishment, or dollar amount will truly be enough. When we put our hope in them to fill us up, to give us purpose and meaning, and call it our identity, well, that's when we find ourselves in a pit of trouble. If we live as if our very essence and value as human beings are determined by what we do, then we've set ourselves up for a life of lonely exhaustion.

We open our Bibles to Matthew 11:28 and read Jesus's words: "Are you tired? Worn out? Burned out on religion?" (MSG).

(I don't think the word "religion" here means going to church or doing church-y things. Instead, it's the never-ending, never quite good enough quest to prove ourselves worthy through our own self-effort.)

Yes, yes! we answer. And we lean in, so weary and wanting, toward this compassionate recognition. We are so hungry for rest.

If Jesus were a modern-day motivational speaker, he'd probably offer this advice: "Well then, try harder! Be more intentional! Create a vision board and follow the 15 steps. Hustle! It's up to you!" If he were a modern-day skeptic, his best advice would be delivered with a hopeless shrug of the shoulders: "Don't let anyone tell you what to do. Quit the hard things. You do you."

I'm poking fun, but it's true, right? These are the mantras of our current culture, and upon reflection, they're the innate impulses within all of us. We either grit our teeth and try harder or give up altogether. Thankfully, Jesus is not bound by our broken ways of doing life, and he offers a third option—a holy invitation freely extended to us whether we're striving or hiding:

> *Come to me. Get away with me and you'll recover your life. I'll show*
> *you how to take a real rest. Walk with me and work with me—watch*
> *how I do it. Learn the unforced rhythms of grace. I won't lay anything*
> *heavy or ill-fitting on you. Keep company with me and you'll learn to*
> *live freely and lightly (Matthew 11:28-30 MSG).*

It's a beautiful invitation, isn't it? So gentle and full of promise, not demanding or critical or based on individual effort. I read this verse at the height of my tiredness and thought to myself, *I want to learn how to recover my life! I want to take a real rest. I don't know what the unforced rhythms of grace are, but they sound wonderful. And more than anything, I wish to live freely and lightly because living bound and heavy is not working out very well.*

Accepting this invitation changed my life. It's not only an invitation to live eternally with him when our time on earth is done, but an invitation into abundant life *now*. We don't have to live from a place of insecurity, self-protection, numbness, and striving. He ushers us out of darkness and into a rich and satisfying life, offering freedom and a secure sense of who he is and who he created us to be. Jesus reorients us so we can live *from* a place of love, purpose, belonging, and identity instead of working *for* these things. He restores us and shows a better way to live, exchanging insecurity for quiet confidence, anxiety for peace. He gives us our identity and purpose, and in response, we gratefully offer our gifts, dreams, and lives back to him for his glory and the good of others.

This book you hold in your hands is my offering. My late thirties were marked by an intense season of healing and spiritual formation with the more dramatic moments culminating around my fortieth birthday. It's been a hard-won battle with the most gracious of outcomes. I have been knocked down, and it has hurt. The last few years have been marked by acts of obedience that might look strange from the outside. My heart, mind, and spirit have been swirling at best and positively churning as I moved through this renewal process. It has required humility as well as a willingness to truly look at myself, to see where I've been trying to earn my worth through self-effort and where I've been burying my head in the sand to ignore the knots in my soul.

There is a fine line between a self-made life and an abundant life, and for a long time, I've been on the self-made side, which leads to burnout and dissatisfaction.

But on the light-filled, abundant side lies a sweet, quiet confidence deep within that I've always longed for. My life circumstances have not improved; in fact, by some standards, things seem worse than before. But my soul is at peace. I can breathe. I no longer have that frantic sense that I'm drowning and it's up to me to keep everything afloat. I have learned that God is good and kind, and he holds us closely in the palm of his very big hand. I've come to trust in his character and believe that what he says of all of us is true: We are his beloved. He deeply values us, and he has made each of us with a glorious purpose

scribble art

so that the world might glimpse how truly great he is.

Spiritual formation is the movement toward becoming more like Jesus and growing into a person of love, joy, and peace; it is a forever process, not a one-time thing. I write my story knowing it is not yet finished and believing that it is covered with grace upon grace. I'm grateful for the growth, humbled by the opportunity to share it with you, and looking forward to the ways God will continue to transform our hearts, minds, and souls as we follow him together.

• • • • •

Never in my wildest childhood dreams would I have imagined that my name would appear on a book as author and illustrator. Only recently have I accepted that I truly am an artist. I suppose that's how a lot of us feel about the gifts we've been given; we think the spotlight is reserved for the more qualified, the better trained, the expert and elite, and all the while, we're missing out on being the people God created us to be.

I didn't want to miss the chance to be that person. And I don't want you to either.

I've tried to pinpoint what this book is exactly, and I can't quite name it. Is it a memoir? Sort of. Jesus invites us to experience abundant life now, and my story is simply an illustration of this greater truth. Is it Christian nonfiction? A little bit. Jesus's words and his vision of us living in his kingdom bring about restoration and freedom, and I can't think of a better topic to write or read about. Is it a pretty coffee-table book to linger over between family activities or tasks in your day for refreshment? That too. I hope that as you and your guests flip through the pages, light will shine, delight will be found, and truth will be revealed.

More than anything, I pray this book is a well-timed gathering of invitations that are so true and tender they cause you to breathe easier. I hope the stories on these pages will help you see more clearly that

you're invited

invitation

your identity is securely set by a trustworthy God, your value does not change based on what you do or don't do, and your best response to his kindness is to use the gifts, talents, passions, and dreams he placed within you as an offering back to him.

● ● ● ● ●

Are you tired? Do you feel a deep unsettledness within? When you look at your life—honestly look and *see*—are you trying to fill or numb a hint of dissatisfaction with your own striving and proving, and it's just not working? Is the question *Who am I?* or *What is my purpose?* or *Am I enough?* on the tip of your tongue, but you're too afraid to speak it into existence? Oh, friend, you are not alone. These questions and feelings, while uncomfortable and disorienting, are so good. Don't push them away! This is God waking you up to abundant life. This is him gently shaking you from the dull slumber of "fine" so you can step across the line into wholehearted freedom. The bravest thing you can do is open up your hands and turn your feet toward the path that leads to new, flourishing growth as you accept Jesus's call to live freely and lightly. It's truly the most beautiful of all invitations.

Xo,

Emily

PART ONE

WE'RE INVITED
TO RECOVER OUR LIVES

dandelion

$\mathcal{N}^{\underline{o}}$ 1

ALL TANGLED UP

I grew up hearing the parable of the sower in Matthew 13, which goes something like this (the Emily paraphrased version):

There once was a farmer who went out to sow seeds. He probably had one of those cute cross-body canvas seed bags, leathery skin, and deep smile lines; at least that's how I imagine him. As he tossed his seeds onto the ground, some of them fell onto a well-traveled road—compact, a bit dusty, but the one everyone took. From high above, the birds saw the good seeds, swooped down, and ate them up. Some seeds fell onto a gravel ditch, and they sprouted quickly. No one was trampling on the ditch, and the birds left it alone, but because the roots could not grow deep, the hot, scorching sun caused the plants to wither and die. Some seeds fell on a path full of thorns and weeds. When the seeds sprouted, so did the weeds, and you know how aggressive weeds can be. But other seeds fell on a path with good, rich soil—the kind you can't resist digging into with your hands. The seeds not only grew into plants but spread and kept producing a harvest year after year after year. Now invite Jesus into your heart, and you'll be like the seeds on that last path.

For most of my Bible-believing life, I would read this story and pat myself on the back while extending sympathy to the people on other paths. *Poor people on paths one, two, and three*, I thought. *I'm so glad I'm on path four.*

But my understanding of this parable was all wrong. It's not just about believing in Jesus (although that's a great place to start). It's about what you *do* with the message of Jesus and what the message of Jesus does to you.

Those on the first path hear the good news about how Jesus replaces their sin with grace, but it doesn't make any sense. As quickly as it is presented, it is plucked away. In one ear, out the other. Those on the second, rocky path gladly hear, but their experience of God's power, provision, and grace remains shallow. When trouble or persecution comes, they're out: *No thank you, this is not for me.* Those on the third path with all those pesky weeds hear the message and they receive it!

Ideal, right? But then their distracted lives, their divided hearts, and their ambition for wealth (Matthew 13:22) take over, and the truth about who Jesus is and what it means to follow him is buried, suffocated. They cannot bear spiritual fruit—the whole love, joy, peace, patience, kindness, goodness, faithfulness, gentleness, and self-control type of fruit. As one Bible translation puts it, "They prefer drunken dinner parties to prayer, power to piety, and riches to righteousness" (Matthew 13:22 THE VOICE). Ouch.

Then there's that fourth and highly desired path, the one on which the travelers hear and fully embrace the truth that God is in charge of their lives, that blessings come from obeying and living according to Jesus's countercultural ways. They find purpose in using their gifts and talents for the good of others and the glory of God.

I thought I was successfully journeying along path four. I sincerely did. I brought my pale-blue Precious Moments Bible to church each Sunday. Taped to the wall of my childhood bedroom were beloved Bible verses written in my best imitation Mary Engelbreit lettering. I went to a Christian college and attended chapel three times each week, spent hours in the tiny prayer chapel on campus, and took Dr. Baloian's popular Life and Teachings of Jesus class. I joined a women's Bible study, and we hosted the young marrieds community group. Our babies were dedicated at the front of the church, and we chose special Bible verses for them. I raised my hands during worship and went forward for prayer when prompted. I even spent a year running the children's program at church because no one else could do it. I was *in* on this Jesus thing. Solidly in.

It turns out you can be solidly in and missing out on abundant life at the same time. As much as my outward actions and earnestness led me to believe I was walking confidently along path four, the soil of my heart looked a lot more like the weed-filled path number three. I was trying with all my might to love God and love people well, but the prickly vines of distraction twisted up around my ankles; dandelion seeds of superficial pleasure danced in the breeze, so harmless looking, so enticing. The worries of the world felt big and urgent, and I was sure it was up to me to do something about them. My divided heart waffled between faith and self-reliance and was making it very difficult to produce all the good, well-developed fruit that's promised for those who abide in Christ. This led me to believe that maybe I wasn't abiding very well. I was definitely saved, but I was not yet free.

These honest realizations are not pleasant to uncover. But just as with any change you want to make, you must first assess yourself and be honest about what comes to light. So that's where we'll start.

Are you tired? What burdens do you carry? How are you responding, and is your response making things better or worse? Jesus in-

GARDENING THINGS

watering can

garden tools

COSMOS

seeds

wheelbarrow

vites us to come to him to recover our lives, but that doesn't feel very compelling unless we can agree that our lives need to be recovered. Maybe you feel as I do—eager to follow Jesus, love, serve, and live well—but in reality, you're caught in a tangle of weeds. You've inadvertently veered onto path three, where worries and a distracted heart make you feel as though your faith is suffocated and fruitless. Instead of the deep peace promised to those who trust in the Lord with all their hearts, you feel anxious and insecure. You wonder, *Is this it? Is this abundant life?*

● ● ● ● ●

Years ago, I bought an old spindle armchair from an estate sale. I fell in love with the lines of the beautifully carved wood legs and the original cane back. The seat, however, was a disaster. The fabric was dingy, stained, and torn. In the middle was a hole with cotton stuffing spilling out. The ties that held the springs in place had long ago broken, which meant they were sticking out at strange angles and made for a very uncomfortable sitting experience. I wasn't too worried about the seat. *I'll just re-cover it*, I thought. I brought the chair home and set to work. I'm a fairly competent DIYer and figured I could put this beauty back together.

I removed the upholstery tacks and took off the old fabric. I

Do not be anxious
about anything,
but in every situation,
by prayer and petition,
with Thanksgiving,
present your requests to God.

PHILIPPIANS 4:6 NIV

straightened the springs and pushed them down. Then I layered on a thick piece of foam and stapled a length of linen fabric tightly around the seat. *Voilà! A new chair!*

Well, sort of. It looked great (if you didn't look too closely at the bulge in the center of the seat), but it was still very uncomfortable to sit on. The springs were stubborn and unwilling to stay firmly coiled. I should have started all over: stripping it down, retying the springs, adding in batting, replacing the webbing. But honestly, that felt like too much effort; so instead, I threw a small sheepskin on top as an extra cushion, and the chair remains in this haphazard state to this day. It looks great pulled up to the head of the dining room table, but when guests come over, I move it into another room; I would never want anyone to actually sit on it!

I wonder how often we tend to our lives in the same way I strove to improve that armchair. We start with a life of beauty and value that is also, if we're honest, a little worn down underneath. We cover up the messy parts to the best of our ability and shove down the awkward, angled broken pieces, hoping the frail places will be forgotten in time. We ignore the obvious flaws, squinting our eyes to make them less noticeable. We say we're fine when, in reality, we're not. We were made in God's image, created to glorify him as we use our lives to reflect his glory back into the world, but it's hard to do this when we're hiding under a hastily done DIY upholstery job.

I know this scenario well. For most of my adulthood, I moved along in the very best way I knew: loving my husband, adoring our four kids, celebrating the creativity I was gifted with, and doing plenty of worthwhile things for God, all the while unaware of just how unsteady my sense of identity was. If an insecurity crept up like a stubborn old spring, I pushed it down, willing it to shush and stay hidden. I looked pretty good from the outside and worked hard to keep up appearances. I operated in the hope that if others saw me as worthy and valuable, I might believe it too. I was not asking God for details about my identity but was trusting in both my own ability and the opinions of others to tell me who I was. I tended to my life with an appearance-focused DIY approach rather than with the spiritual work of honest exploration, listening, truth telling, stripping down, and restoring from the bones up.

In order for my antique chair to serve its intended purpose as a pleasant place to sit, the fabric and batting have to come off, and the inner workings need care from a professional who can bring it back to its original

chair

glory. The same is true of my life. Maybe it's true of your life as well. No amount of reshuffling schedules, prioritizing self-care, mustering up the strength, and putting on a brave face will ever end in true healing, satisfaction, and restoration. We can't possibly live lives of joy, peace, and love while we're distracted, anxious, and unsure of who we are and searching for significance in superficial places. The inner workings of our hearts must be reset by the only One who can recover them back to their original glory.

One dictionary defines the word "recover" as "to get back again: regain. To regain normal health, poise, or status." Jesus doesn't invite us to throw something pretty over our hearts and call it good enough. Instead, as we come to him, he fully *reclaims* our purpose and identity. He takes our lives—our beautiful, dinged-up lives—and restores them to complete wholeness, full of hope, freedom, and rest. No matter what path we are walking on, Jesus's answer is so simple: "Come to me. Get away with me and you'll recover your life" (Matthew 11:28-30 MSG).

Does your life need to be recovered? Are you tired of relying on your own effort and the opinions of others to feel worthy? When insecurities creep up, do you keep pushing them down? Are you saved but not yet free? Jesus stands at the ready to begin the work of recovering your life.

alarm clock

$\mathcal{N}\!\!\underline{\circ}$ 2

WAKING UP ON A BUS

I didn't know my life needed to be recovered. I thought I was doing okay. I was a 35-year-old mom of four with all the outward things working for me: a supportive husband, healthy kids, a pretty house in a neighborhood with manicured lawns, and a big group of friends. We belonged to a growing church. I had a popular blog and a profitable small business filled with creative endeavors. It was everything I ever wanted—even better than I could have dreamed up myself. At least that's what I thought until the day I woke up on a bus in Rwanda.

All my life I had wanted to go to Africa—full of smiling people with colorful clothing and exotic languages, cultures, and animals. It felt so far outside my American norm. My heart always skipped a beat and my eyes welled up when my church showed a video of Africa or visiting missionaries described its most burdened areas. I felt compelled to help. To serve. To see the beauty and devastation for myself. So when the opportunity arose to go to Rwanda, I quickly replied with a resounding yes.

● ● ▪ ● ◖

This trip to Rwanda wasn't a mission trip; it was an influencer tour created in honor of the twentieth anniversary of the genocide to bring awareness to the incredible work of International Justice Mission (IJM) and Noonday Collection, a fair-trade jewelry company that partners with artisans worldwide. Those invited were a combination of big names in the Christian author/speaker/ministry space, two top-selling Noonday ambassadors, representatives from the IJM team, one delightful young woman who won inclusion through a social campaign, and me, a lifestyle blogger. We were modern-day "journalists" reporting on the efforts to aid the country's recovery and illuminating how people could contribute to this noble cause.

Each morning, we rose from our mosquito-netted beds, piled on our colorful Noonday jewelry, and climbed the concrete stairs to the top floor of the small but lovely hotel for expertly made lattes and a buffet breakfast of exotic fruits and jellies and very dry toast. We ate on the patio under red umbrellas, where we learned our itinerary each day. Our week was packed with meaningful experiences: fellowshipping with a prayer group of women who had been sexually abused, sewing with the co-op ladies, visiting homes, walking somberly through genocide sites, and celebrating the new home of an IJM lawyer who survived the genocide as a boy and was now fighting for justice in his beloved country. Our days were full, and it was such an honor to be part of all of it.

Despite the big names and even bigger personalities on the trip, there were no big egos or comparison dramas or annoying cliques.

latte

Everyone was kind, inclusive, interested in each other, and passionate about the work we were doing. Each time we entered the bus to travel to and from the daily adventures, we swapped seats, chatting to get to know each other, quieting as we processed the day, white-knuckling the seats in front of us as our driver swerved to dodge potholes and pedestrians and the occasional cow on the country roads.

Midway through the week, as we wrapped up another day filled with equal amounts of heartache and hope, we boarded the bus heading to downtown Kigali for dinner. I was first on the bus and took a seat a few rows back. The rest of the team followed. Our little bus filled up until everyone had chosen their spots and the hum of conversation began. The seat beside me remained empty.

The sudden salty tears and the lonely ache in my chest took me by surprise. I knew crying about this was completely ridiculous. I could have blamed it on the raw emotions of missing my family or the hard realities we were witnessing each day, but honestly, I was just devastatingly sad that no one chose to sit next to me. *What is wrong with me?* I internalized, head in hands, shoulders shaking. *Why doesn't anyone want to sit with me? Am I not interesting enough? Am I not funny or popular or noteworthy enough? Am I too introspective and boring?* A deep well of long-ignored insecurities surfaced, and the triggered emotions were uncontainable

• • ▸ • ◆

A few days before, I had overheard one of the most beloved women on the team say something about how she was not friends with precious lambs. She didn't do sensitive, gentle-souled people. She needed sturdy, boisterous, speak-your-mind friends. I am, without a doubt, a precious lamb. And in that moment on the bus, I not only felt like a crybaby precious lamb; I felt like that missing sheep from the Bible story—the one the shepherd leaves the ninety-nine to go find. Except in my version, no one even noticed I was gone. I was overlooked, unnoticed, forgotten, insignificant, rejected.

At dinner that night, a sweet friend gathered me in and asked me questions, trying to find the source of the blurry eyes and the messed-up mascara. As I shared my story—my entire life story, poor thing—she said something I'll never forget: "It sounds like everything in your life right now is fine. But what if there is better?" That simple question struck something deep within me, and I ask it to you now: *What if there is better?*

We know instinctively that *better* doesn't refer to stuff. We know that filling our houses with more knickknacks and filling our bellies with more food won't make things better. We know we can't add meaning and purpose to our lives by endlessly scrolling online, binge-watching the latest show, and keeping hectic after-school

lamb

schedules. Better is not about amassing more clothes or having a nicer house. It isn't secured through a fancier job title or a more perfect soul mate. A better life is not promised to those who get into the right school or have the right group of friends or never sit alone on a bus. Better is not found in having more. It's not even found in having less (sorry, minimalists of the world). It's not in the externals at all.

And yet...

It's so tempting to look to all this good stuff to make us happy. Our jobs, our relationships, our kids, our pretty houses, the joy-sparking decluttering, and who can forget those revolving Amazon deliveries? Well, that's what I was focused on at least. This was the good life, and I was all about it. In the beginning, I knew these good things were merely good *things*, yet slowly, without even noticing, the good things became *everything*. They gave me my identity, my value, my title, significance, and status. My arms were outstretched, grabbing and pulling it all close; I was possessive and proud of all I could call mine. I was choking the good things to death, trying to make them serve my needs, asking them to satisfy and define me when they should never have that power. The trappings of the good life had me trapped.

● ◆ ▪ ◆ ◆

The pursuit of keeping what I had and getting more of what I didn't distracted me from the hurts and insecurities lurking under the surface. At first glance, I looked like I had it all together, but right underneath, I was a wounded, tender, terrified, precious lamb who couldn't hold it together anymore.

That's how it goes, it seems. We all come to that point at a certain age or season, or we encounter a life event that forces us to face the reality that the life we've created for ourselves is not everything we imagined it would be. We look around at all the good things (and they truly are good!) and still have a gnawing dissatisfaction. We're tempted to blame all the externals: *Maybe if I had better friends. Maybe if my house was bigger or freshly remodeled or less messy or in a different city. Maybe if my bank account had an extra zero or I had more time or could get more sleep. Surely then things would be better.*

We elevate happiness as the greatest virtue and believe we are in charge of our own happiness, so if we're unhappy, well, it's up to us to fix it. So we work harder. We people-please. We chase dreams and hustle, moving from one thing to the next, always searching for purpose and significance only to be left disappointed, unsettled, unsatisfied. And exhausted.

When we look at ourselves from the outside, we might see an Instagram-perfect life. But inside? Inside, it's not quite so pretty. Or sharable. Questions and doubts and fears and anxieties are stuffed down in our dark places, because who wants to deal with any of this?

We push away the uncomfortable feelings and pretend like they aren't there, moving along the way we've always gone, hoping that ignorance truly is bliss.

I lived in such denial until that one day on the other side of the world when I sat on a bus suddenly aware of just how insecure I truly was. That is when I awakened to this truth: *I wanted better but was searching for it in all the wrong places.*

$$\bullet \quad \bullet \quad \bullet \quad \bullet \quad \bullet$$

I was compelled to go to Africa under the pretense that I could do some heroic helping, but in fact, I needed to go to Africa to be saved. My vision of the good life and my unwavering dedication to achieving it was inadvertently robbing me of true freedom and abundant life. I was bound by self-effort and insecurity, dependent on being constantly chosen and approved of. I didn't know I needed to reclaim my place on the path toward true identity and purpose until that moment. That's how sneaky our own deception can be. That's also how good we get at distancing ourselves from our broken places and our need for God.

The journey to better, to the peace-filled existence Jesus invites us to, requires us to willingly face the hidden parts inside that can't be healed by continued avoidance or a new pair of shoes, well-behaved children, meeting a business goal, or a tropical vacation. I think that's what my friend was getting at that night at dinner in Rwanda. "Emily, what if digging into all of your insecurities and questions could result in something even greater than you could imagine? Maybe it's time to let go of 'fine.'" Of course, she was right.

I ask the same question of you: What if admitting your insecurities and asking yourself the hard questions could result in a life better than you could imagine? Jesus extends an open-armed invitation to all of us who are burdened to come to him with the promise that he will draw us close and restore us to wholeness. The transformation starts with a humble awakening to the truth that he is indeed better. Is it time, my friend, to wake up to what's better and get away with Jesus to recover your life?

For he satisfies
the longing soul,
and the hungry soul
he fills with good things.

PSALM 107:9 ESV

champagne

$\mathcal{N}_{\underline{o}}$ 3

I'M FINE (I'M NOT FINE)

A trendy and meaningful way to ring in the new year is to choose a special word. It might represent what you hope for in the upcoming year or something you've been pondering lately. It could be a character trait you'd like to focus on or a phrase to keep you motivated long after the confetti has been cleaned up and you're back to normal life. I'm admittedly not great at making resolutions. Big-picture, forward thinking is not my greatest gift. Add to this my great disdain for unmet expectations, and you have a girl who isn't much into setting goals. But the New Year's word thing I can get behind.

The year after visiting Rwanda, my husband, Ryan, and I decided to each choose words for the new year and set a date to share them. In my romanticized imagination, I pictured us sitting across from one other, the glow of firelight flickering, soft music playing in the background, eyes locked on each other, wine in hand. On the count of three, we would softly offer our words, and like true soul mates, those words we spoke would be the same. We would smile knowing smiles, kiss tenderly, and walk hand in hand into the sunset and toward our happily ever after. End scene. (I admit I've watched too many romantic comedies.)

I'm sure you'll be shocked to find out it didn't happen that way.

First of all, our fireplace was that kind that turned on with a light switch, and it never gave off much heat or ambiance. Second, eye gazing is weird. And third, I don't really like wine.

In reality, our sharing of our new-year words played out like this: We stood at the kitchen island, the kids finally in bed and dinner dishes drip-drying next to the sink, and one of us chimed in, "Oh yeah! We forgot to tell each other our words!"

I went first: *Settled*.

Ryan laughed and then followed: *BAD****.

It's true; that was his word. Not something fluffy and sweet, not something catchy you get made into a wooden sign for the wall in your office, and certainly not the same as mine. In fact, it was the complete *opposite* of mine. If I was going for calm, comfortable, and sure, he was after exciting and bold—a true shakeup.

I have a strong desire to be normal: to do things like I'm supposed to, to be on my best behavior, and to act according to expectations with a smile on my face. *Gain approval, avoid disappointment, and all will be well,* that's what I say. In a preschool class photo among boys and girls with tousled hair, scuffed shoes, goofy grins, and slouching posture, I sit up tall in the center. I'm unfazed by the chaos around me, my head slightly tilted, my hair in perfect ringlets, my white cotton tights smooth and clean, and my hands folded gently in my lap. Even at age four, I was keenly aware of the pressure of appearances.

The word "settled" did not express a new desire for me; it has always been my go-to wish. I like peace (or at least my shallower understanding of it—the absence of conflict) and tried my very best to keep the surface of my life tidy and attractive in an attempt to make the deeper parts of me believe it was true. To feel settled would mean everything was fine, and even though there were clear glimpses that this was not the case, like the stubborn redhead that I am, I was determined to force things to at least appear that way.

You know that feeling when a friend calls to let you know she is in the neighborhood and asks to drop by? Of course you say yes, but up until that very last second when the doorbell rings, you're shoving all the clutter into the hall closet, hoping she won't notice the random socks sticking out from under the door. *I'm fine. Everything's fine. See how fine everything appears?* I'm an expert at this.

I get this whole gloss-over gumption from my grandma. When my uncle, her firstborn, was diagnosed with Lou Gehrig's disease with a short life expectancy, we gathered as a family to pray for miraculous healing. A few minutes in, with tissues passed and sweet vulnerability thick in the air, my dry-eyed grandma stood up from her place on the couch, clapped her hands, and called the prayer time over. Time to talk about something else. *Anything* else: "We won't babble on about this anymore. He's going to be fine."

Somewhere along the way, many of us learn that it's easier to either bury our heads in the sand or sweep anything unsightly or uncomfortable under the rug, to pretend the issues aren't there. For as long as I can remember, I watched my grandma put on a good fuchsia-lipsticked face, staying resolutely positive and always hyperaware of what everyone would think. This is how she lived her life. And from my perspective, it looked pretty wonderful. She was well liked, social, the most generous hostess, and always touting her family's newest

THINGS THAT REMIND ME OF GRANDMA

lipstick

black coffee

antique ring

playing cards

orange slice candy

Socks

success to whoever was joining her for coffee on the porch that day. But if she asked you to rub out the tight spot on her back, it was like putting hands to concrete; the muscles were knotted and hard. I wonder if all those years of holding everything together so tightly weighed heavily upon her shoulders, never to be released until the day she went home to be with the Lord. Now, if her back felt like this, what did the very deepest, most vulnerable hidden parts of her feel like? Burdened, heavy, tangled, ever responsible, bound? I adore many things about my grandma, but this stubborn desire to keep everything "fine" is not one of them.

• • • • •

Over the course of a year, I began to wake up how my pursuit of *settled* bound me. Like my grandma, I was trading the deeply rooted true peace of wholeness, security, and well-being for shallow appearances. For the first time, I clearly saw my life and my way of being, and I didn't like it. The covering up and ignoring that had become second nature was now becoming uncomfortable and obvious. The hall closet of my soul was starting to bulge with all the junk I had crammed in there with the hope it would all just disappear. Some metaphorical stray socks were starting to show.

We all have our own struggles, and at the time, I was doing the best I knew how. I don't need to shame the Emily of this era, but I certainly want to learn from her. What we give our attention to shapes our thinking and trains our affections. I held a lot of unhelpful beliefs that were turning me into a person I never meant to be.

I spent night and day tiptoeing on eggshells, trying to do all I could to make Ryan happy, ever fearful of disappointing him. *If I am perfect*, I thought, *if I keep the house clean and the kids well behaved, if I apologize first and am agreeable and attractive, then he will find me worthy.* His approval of me meant *everything*, and I never felt like I could get enough of it. This, of course, is a terrible way to approach a marriage partnership and an equally disastrous place to search for true identity. Ryan chose to marry me and love me, and aside from the normal two-people-living-under-one-roof types of disagreements, he never once let on that he was disappointed in his choice to share his last name and life with me. But that didn't stop me from doubting his love and acceptance.

I avoided any conversation that felt like conflict, even with the people closest to me (*especially* with the people closest to me), playing that all-familiar game of sucking up my feelings when they were legitimately hurt. I just closed my mouth, dealt with it in my own heart, and moved on as if nothing happened. But deep down, I felt dismissed and unimportant, which fueled the belief that maybe I was to blame and made me try harder to gain approval and avoid disappointing anyone.

My expectations were out of control. There was no way I could be the kind of mom, wife, friend, and woman I pressured myself to be, and as a result, I felt like a failure in pretty much every way. Even when my husband, kids, friends, and online community told me I was great, the critical inner voice bossing me around was louder and more influential. It told me to get my act together and prove to the world that I was enough.

Over time, it became impossible to sustain my efforts to create a life that looked good on the outside and hide what wasn't fine. Worst of all, I didn't like who I was becoming. In an effort to keep life smooth and settled, I had turned into a self-deprecating control freak, desperate for attention and afraid of failing. Without realizing it, I had forgotten who I truly was, and I was hurting the people I loved the most in the process. Despite what I so desperately wanted to believe, I wasn't fine. I longed for a settled spirit but was going about it the wrong way. Ryan's new-year word was much more accurate for what true healing would look like. I needed a shake-up to be set free to find the deep wholeness, lasting peace, and true security I so longed for.

● ◆ ◗ ● ◗

We each have our own mixed-up concoction of beliefs and behaviors that have carried us through life. At this point in the invitation to abundant life, I urge you to deeply look at yourself and your beliefs— to clear away the fog of familiarity and pay attention. Do you like what you see? Are you becoming who you want to become? Are you pursuing what you want to pursue? Are you stubbornly holding on to "fine" like I was? Are you looking to relationships, material possessions, or achievements to prove your worth? How are you *genuinely* doing?

Don't forget Jesus's promise: "Come to me. Get away with me and you'll recover your life."

It's okay to admit you are not fine. In fact, it's the first step to freedom.

Window box

And we all,
who with unveiled faces
contemplate the Lord's glory,
are being transformed
into his image
with ever-increasing glory,
which comes from the Lord,
who is the Spirit.

2 CORINTHIANS 3:18 NIV

starfish

No. 4

WHO AM I?

I sat alone on the warm sand. With my arms tightly hugging my knees, I listened to the rhythmic crashing of the waves. In and out. In and out. The cadence slowed my breath, and its low roar drowned out all other noise. In front of me, the deep blue ocean spilled over into the horizon in the distance. The swimmers and surfers and sunbathers had gone in for the day; the beach was dotted with only a few remaining vacationers. There was little to distract me. No one to impress. Nowhere to be. It was quiet, alive, powerful.

My heart was burdened, tangled into a messy knot that was getting tighter every day. I should have been with Ryan or the group of friends we were vacationing with, but I could no longer bear the weight of the never-ending pressures, looming sadness, and gnawing disappointment. I needed to be alone, to cry and think and finally surrender. My body was still as I stared out into the vastness before me, but inside it was a jumble of questions and worries, all wrapped up in prayer. I felt so small sitting there on the beach but also so *seen*.

You know how Google Earth does that cool, fast zoom to the location you put in—say, the Eiffel Tower or the Great Sphinx of Giza? That's how I visualized being noticed. Spotted. Found. I was the location. Imagine the rotating sphere of planet Earth floating in star-splattered darkness, growing larger, moving closer, coming into focus. The continents take shape, with the blues of the waters and the greens and browns of the land. It moves closer and closer, spinning smoothly until finally slowing to a stop in the middle of the Pacific Ocean and zooming in on a pinprick of a spot right there on a tiny volcanic island where a pale-skinned woman sits, her arms folded around herself, finally brave and still enough to ask the hardest question she's ever asked.

Who am I?

I had lost myself. In the striving, the proving, the working, the loving and serving and giving, the attempt to hold it all together, the kids and job and house, the volunteering, the church activities and neighborhood gatherings, the worries and hurts, the good and bad choices, the messy and beautiful, I had lost sight of who I was. I know that sounds weird. I mean, of course I know who I am. I am Emily.

globe

Daughter, sister, mom, wife, writer, artist. I have red hair and a toe on my right foot that curls under. I sneeze when I look at the sun. I don't eat oatmeal or chicken on the bone, but I'll try most anything else. When my iron levels get low, I chew ice. Sleeping in is my favorite. I prefer jeans to dresses, neutrals to color. I'm delighted by flowers and will shake like crazy if my coffee is not decaf. I have nice handwriting and love children. These things are all true about me. But that wasn't quite it.

Who am I *really*? If my hair turned from red to gray or my husband left me or I quit blogging or I suddenly started enjoying oatmeal (terribly unlikely, but we'll go with it for the sake of the illustration), who would I be? If all the externals are blurred out of focus and the only thing remaining is the very core of who I am, stripped bare of the titles, labels, stories, masks, and makeup, who is *that* girl?

And the next scary question: Is she enough?

Who am I? I whisper-cried aloud to the ocean before me. I knew this moment would come. It was only a matter of time.

• ◆ ▸ ◆ ◉

When Mason, our third son, was four years old, he developed a bad habit of hitting. He's sweet and spunky and by far the most physical of the three boys, a characteristic that makes sense as he's the little brother who is always trying to keep up. His unbecoming behavior didn't happen at his preschool or with his brothers; mostly he just hit me. How nice. This alter-ego version of him would show up out of nowhere and pound me in the leg with his little fist. Instead of a gentle goodnight kiss, he'd wave his arms all around, inevitably catching my shoulder or cheek with his wild hands. When I tried to high-five him, this kid threw his fist into my palm. The response hurt physically and emotionally. I was confused and concerned.

I did all the right behavioral modification techniques: I got down at eye level to explain that hitting Mommy was unacceptable. He spent time-outs on the stairs. He lost privileges. Nothing worked. I talked to a social worker friend who counseled high-risk teens, and she suggested that I take him to a counselor to talk about anger issues. I couldn't understand why he was hitting me, but my mother's intuition told me it wasn't anger.

While praying about my baby one morning, I had a flash of God-given clarity. Every time he hit me, instead of reacting, I would gather him into my arms for a hug. I stood at the open fridge later that morning, and up came Mason with his fists at the ready. Instead of growing frustrated, I smiled at him, wrapped my arms around his squirming, pajama-clad body, and snuggled him tight. He tried to wiggle out of it, but I held on just long enough to tell him I loved him, and I said something silly about how every time he hit me, it must mean that he needed a hug.

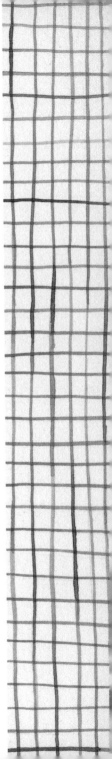

And you know what? He *did* need a hug. All along, his hitting was his very messed-up way of letting me know that he felt forgotten and needed to be reassured of my love.

It's tempting to look at an outward action and assume it's just a behavior in need of correction. We create boundaries and expectations for improved, acceptable behavior, but when we fail to look deeper, we may miss what's actually going on. Perhaps with enough time-outs and lost privileges, Mason would have stopped hitting, but I would have missed his tender heart under the bad behavior. Our middle child just needed to know he was loved and not forgotten, and he didn't know how else to tell me.

In many ways, I was just like my little Mason. Sure, some unbecoming behavioral issues in my life needed to be resolved, but if I had only stopped at the surface and modified my outward actions with goal setting and rulemaking, I would have missed what was happening underneath. All my mixed-up efforts to seek approval and control the outward appearance of my life were my poor attempts to find the answer to the deeper heart questions: Am I significant, loved, and not forgotten?

When you peer under the surface of your behavior, are you, too, a little bit like Mason? Are you trying to find out who you are and if it is enough? If so, then you're in good company.

• ◆ ▪ • ◆

Sitting on that serene Hawaiian beach with my hair caught up in the ocean breeze and my breath slowing to the rhythm of the tide, I felt both surprisingly courageous and utterly exhausted. I had finally laid my wounded heart wide open in surrender. *I am so tired. I am trying so hard to hold everything together, to prove that I'm okay. It's not working. I can't keep doing this. Lord, I can't keep doing this.*

A light, warm rain began to fall. I turned to glance at the view behind me, and right above the lush green Hawaiian foothills, a rainbow appeared. A rainbow sighting always feels exciting, especially when you've just poured your heart out and told the very bravest truth with all your broken heart to a God you hope heard you. I'd like to think that rainbow was a way for God to speak what I desperately needed to hear in that moment:

> *I see you. I have not forgotten you. And I'm right here with you now. You might not know who you are anymore, but I do. It's time to heal, to tell the truth, to stop trying to fill yourself with things that weren't made to satisfy. You are worshipping the wrong things. Come to Me, you who are weary and heavily burdened, and I will give you rest.*

He said this to me, and he says it to you too. He sees you right now, whether you are sitting on a tropical beach, snuggled on the couch, or

where can I go from your Spirit?
where can I flee from your presence?
If I go up to the heavens,
   you are there;
If I make my bed in the depths,
   you are there.
If I rise on the wings of the dawn,
If I settle on the far side of the sea,
even there your hand will guide me,
your right hand will hold me fast.

PSALM 139:7-10 NIV

in your car in the school pick-up line. He has not forgotten you. He is jealous for your heart.

Are you tired? Worn out? Burnt out on all the striving, the filling, the searching? Are you sick of hearing that nagging voice that plays the same accusations again and again—quietly on some days, full blast on others? *Try harder. Prove your worth. It's up to you. It's your fault. You're not enough.*

Jesus wraps his arms around you, so much less concerned with your bad behavior than your precious heart. "Come to me," he says. "Get away with me and you'll recover your life."

rainbow

PART TWO

WE'RE INVITED
TO TAKE A REAL REST

hydrangea

$\mathcal{N}^{\underline{o}}$ 5

PRUNING PLANTS AND PURGING CLOSETS

In front of our house sits a huge hydrangea plant that's blooming like crazy right now. Every time a friend comes over, I send her home with an armful of the perfect purply-blue blossoms with plenty more on the bush to spare. My favorite black-and-white striped pitcher, overflowing with big hydrangea stems, sits in the center of my kitchen table. The kids keep moving it at dinnertime because we can't see each other over it, but I move it back once we're finished because few things make me happier than fresh flowers.

Last year, our hydrangea had only a few blooms, but this year, it's a different story. What changed? In the fall, Ryan pruned the shrub way back. It pained me to see him cut away my beloved hydrangea, my favorite flower! It's what my bridesmaids carried in my wedding and one of the things that drew me to our new house in the first place.

It felt so wrong to take off so much. What if the cutting back meant the shrub would never bloom again?

But as it turns out, pruning is exactly what that hydrangea plant needed in order to flourish. I don't know a ton about gardening, but I do know that pruning is part of the deal. Old limbs and dried blossoms are removed. A shrub is clipped into a shape like a squared-off hedge or topiary or a giant boxwood elephant sculpture. Sometimes there are so many offshoots and crisscrossing branches, the poor thing can't figure out where to send nutrients. Unless some are cleared out, the whole plant suffers. It's not always about cutting off the old and the dead though; at times perfectly fine parts are removed for the sake of the plant and its ongoing health and potential to thrive. With each cut, growth is stopped in one direction and encouraged in another.

After Jesus invites us to come to him to recover our lives, he extends a second invitation, this time a promise: "I will give you rest" (Matthew 11:28 NIV). I believe in self-care and rest. I don't know a single person who would pass on the chance to spend an afternoon doing only the most enjoyable and calming activities. Let yourself daydream about a perfectly restful scenario. It looks delightful, doesn't it? When I think of rest, I imagine a midafternoon nap, a break from responsibility, time to paint or bake or read uninterrupted. Yet when I read Jesus's amazing offer to show us how to take a *real* rest, I wonder if

candle

there is a difference between his version and mine, if he has something deeper and more lasting in mind than a long bubble bath by the light of a favorite Anthropologie candle.

• • • • •

My mom loves shopping. Scratch that—my mom loves a good deal. This is great when it comes to making wise purchasing decisions, like waiting for a couch to go on sale or scouring Craigslist for gently used American Girl dolls for her granddaughters instead of buying them brand new. But take a look at her overflowing closet and you'll quickly see that a markdown on a price tag has tempted her one too many times.

Last year, she asked my sisters and me to come help her purge her cluttered closet. My older sister, Amy, like a true firstborn, is organized and has a gracious way of telling the truth without hurting feelings. Hillary, my little sister, is the fashionable one, and we all look to her for opinions on what to wear. And me? Well, I'm just very good at getting rid of things.

We met up at Mom's house on a Friday morning and set right to work. One by one, we pulled items out of her closet, asking a set of quick decision-making questions: *Do you wear it? Do you like it? Does it fit?* If she couldn't answer yes to all three questions, the sweater or dress or pair of pants was tossed to the side. By the end of Operation Closet Clean Out, my mom's wardrobe was cut in half and her closet was lovingly organized with only the clothes, shoes, and bags she needed and wanted. Mission accomplished. This day of purging was painful for my nostalgic, deal-seeking mom. She had an attachment to almost every article of clothing, and even if it was never worn or no longer in style, it had a memory or a sale price that she didn't want to part with. She put up a playful fight with each piece that landed in the growing giveaway pile, finally acquiescing as we reminded her that she asked for this.

The clearing out, while hard, was so good. It made room on the racks, provided space for her clothes to hang nicely, and revealed to my mom that just because it was a good deal did not mean it needed to be *her* good deal. The purging of the overstuffed closet was necessary to clear away the old and the unflattering and leave open space for future can't-pass-up purchases.

· · · · ·

The pruning of plants and purging of closets can feel unsettling and stir up fear: What if cutting away means nothing good will grow back in its place? What if I never find another dress as wondersful (even though it's the wrong size)? Most of us don't readily invite change, endings, and loss into our lives. These are hard to endure and even harder to welcome. But as my wise friend Reagan says, "An element of disruption is always needed to initiate lasting change." My soul was ready for lasting change.

Real rest requires an undoing. Like removing your shoes before tucking your legs up under you on the couch or taking out your ponytail before laying your head down, the things that are binding and tangling

Scissors

need to be unbound and untangled to prepare for real, deep, spiritual rest. This is no small act.

As we accept Jesus's invitation to find real rest, we have to start with surrender. When we release our tight grip on our lives, we allow old patterns and wrong ways of thinking to fall away. There's no difference between pruning an unfruitful branch and letting go of the blouse that never did fit right. This letting go makes way for new, beautiful, abundant growth.

Uncovering what we need to release from our lives and figuring out how to loosen our grip on them takes time, patience, and intentional effort. As I began to pay attention to the behaviors and patterns of being that kept me in a hamster wheel of striving, I identified a few big ones: Control. Comparison. Distractions. Comfort. And an overall reliance on self. These parts had to be cut away. I knew it would hurt, but ultimately, I held firmly to the hope that Jesus's invitation into real rest was for me, and this was a necessary step in receiving it.

Sleeping in, time alone, coffee with friends, and finding hobbies that make you come alive are all wonderful. Do these things! But don't just stop there. The rest Jesus offers is *true* rest for our souls that we can find only when we let go of unfruitful efforts to prove ourselves worthy and make room for God to bring forth new life. We participate in this growth by letting go of our mistaken beliefs about where identity, purpose, and belonging are found and allow him to restore our hearts to the truth. Are you longing for a deep inner disposition of rest? If so, it's freely yours.

grapes

He cuts off every branch in me
that bears no fruit,
while every branch that does
bear fruit he prunes
so that it will be
even more fruitful.

JOHN 15:2 NIV

mailbox

$\mathcal{N}\underline{o.}$ 6

BE STILL

A package was stuffed into our mailbox when I went to check for mail. It was from a dear friend whom I haven't done a great job of staying in touch with now that we live in separate cities and have husbands and kids. I was eager to see what was inside.

Carefully encased in layers of bubble wrap was an old picture frame she found while unpacking boxes in their new house. "Be still, and know that I am God," read the artwork inside. I instantly recognized it.

I made the piece for her in 1999, and it traveled with her from college in Chicago back to her parent's house, to the apartment building where we both lived while newlyweds, and then to each of her next homes. In the note accompanying this surprise gift, she expressed hope I wasn't offended that she had sent it back to me, but when she came across it recently, she sensed she needed to.

I was grateful for the well-timed return of this treasure.

The verse "Be still, and know that I am God" (Psalm 46:10 NIV) is well loved and often quoted in times of struggle or worry about the unknown. We usually read it from the perspective of a gentle father patting his fretful child reassuringly on the head: *Shhh, child. Settle down. I will take care of you.* And I'm pretty sure that's exactly the meaning I had in mind all those years ago when I created the little painting. I think God probably does whisper those words to our troubled hearts at times.

But as I was in this new season of uncovering the unpleasant realities of my insecure identity and owning up to the ways I was errantly depending on self-effort, the words "Be still" took on a new (and probably more contextually accurate) meaning: *Stop striving. Surrender your anxiety. Be in awe of me. I am in charge of your protection, and I am more powerful than any nation or trouble or worry. Your efforts are getting in the way, and you're making it harder than it needs to be. Move to the side; I've got this. Trust me.*

The tone is a little less gentle daddy and more powerful protector, isn't it? He's in charge, not me, and maybe I'm not quite as helpful as I think I am.

• ◆ ▪ ◆ ◆

Be still,
and know that
I am God.

PSALM 46:10 NIV

I've recently spent some time reading stories from the Old Testament and have had to accept a surprising truth: I have a lot in common with the Israelites and the way they handled change and control.

They were rescued by God. They honored and worshipped him. All good, right? But after a while, they began to question his ways. They saw trouble and worried about where they would get food and how they would make it to the promised land. Since God wasn't moving fast enough, they took matters into their own hands. They chose to worship pagan gods and aligned with military powers they thought would protect them. They exchanged trust in God for trust in their own intellect, insight, and ideas.

It sounds eerily familiar. God saved me, and I honored and worshipped him. Eventually I started to see gaps between what I wanted in life and what I had. I might not have said it outright, but inside me lingered the belief that God wasn't doing it right. I didn't leave him completely; I just found new gods to worship alongside him to fill in the gaps. They weren't the rudimentary carved images from ancient times. Instead, mine were refined, sophisticated little gods, like relationships, appearance, treasures, and my accomplishments that offered identity, meaning, and purpose outside of my identity as a child of God. I aligned with popular cultural norms and used my abilities and insights to avoid pain and make life as happy and trouble-free as possible.

Just like the Israelites, I held tightly to control, and my efforts were wearing me out. God gave me gifts to care for and enjoy, but I was using them to give me value. I needed my husband's constant approval, a picture-perfect house, a busy social calendar, a regular routine, increasing finances, and a polished appearance to provide meaning and value, to tell me I was safe, loved, significant, enough. My striving left me exhausted and surprisingly dissatisfied with a life so full of good things. My desires made everything in my life lopsided. From the beginning, God was after my heart, but my heart needed to be still for a minute so I could sort out this control thing.

• • • • •

When you live in a big family, the laundry situation can become quite an ordeal. I know I should just transfer the responsibility onto the kids; they are surely old enough to manage washing and folding their own clothes, and sometimes I encourage this. It's just that I have a *system*, and I like my system. I like to wash and dry the clothes and then pile them on the couch on an evening when the kids are in bed and Ryan is working late in his home office. It provides the perfect multitasking excuse to catch up on the latest episode of my favorite reality show, *Project Runway*.

In this long-running reality show, a handful of up-and-coming

laundry

fashion designers compete each week to create unbelievable garments in only a few days with a limited budget. The creative genius that comes from these brilliant minds and hands is something to behold. As I neatly fold and stack the mountain of laundry I've saved for this TV-watching moment, I'm thoroughly entertained by each episode's challenge. I'm especially captivated when the designers are given reasonable budgets and freedom to do their thing, and I cringe along with them when it's announced that this time, they'll draw a button from the bag to see who their partner will be. Ugh. Group projects are the *worst*. You have to collaborate, consider, and compromise. You have to give up control. It is very clear which teams will be successful and which ones will struggle based on how much contestants cling to their own ways. I'm afraid that if I were on the show, I'd make a lousy partner.

In my school days, group projects were not my forte. I tried to listen to everyone's ideas and come up with a paper or presentation that incorporated all our best offerings, but it was hard. Most of the time, I was that girl who took over, writing the whole paper or finishing the poster on my own because, honestly, I wasn't sure anyone else would do it right. And I could not imagine putting my grades and reputation in the hands of anyone other than capable old me.

If asked if I'm picky, I'll answer no. That's not my style of control.

I like to be flexible and open minded, and I hope most people find that I'm easy and pleasant to be around. But ask me if I'm *particular*, and that's a different story. I'm particular about how the dishwasher is loaded because obviously the bowls fit best on the lower right rack. I'm particular about the sleeves of the T-shirts facing the same direction when folded so they stack nicely. I'm particular about eating my food while it's piping hot, and I get a little grouchy when I have to wait at the dinner table for my less temperature-concerned family members to arrive. I'm particular about practically every aspect of my work that might reflect back onto me: graphics, emails, packaging, branding. I'm particular about how the kids look when we go out, especially when we take family photos.

Being particular is normal. We all have our preferences. It's when those particularities become cemented in our minds as the *only* way that they cross over to the arena of control. Ouch, right? Control is especially ugly when I prioritize my own preferences over my care for another person. It's what happens when I rearrange the dishwasher, huffing under my breath about my son's incompetency in doing it right. It's the urge to take over when my daughter is not folding her clothes properly (this is why I insist on folding myself!) and the self-righteousness that comes out when I take a bite before we all gather to pray because *I just spent all this time making this food, and*

I want to eat it while it's hot. It's the overworked and stressed-out outcome of not asking for help or trusting another person to do what I mistakenly think only I can do and not caring if a sweater is itchy or a pair of pants is uncomfortable because *it is what I want you to wear, and you will wear it.*

My preferences are usually harmless, but they can creep in quietly, and soon enough I find myself being particular about more than just the day-to-day things, like promptness and how the pillows are arranged on the couch. Instinctively, my eyes search and my hands grasp for opportunities to express *my* way. Control makes me feel powerful, and I like feeling powerful. It puts me and my great ideas in charge, and I think my ideas are pretty great. It allows me to be responsible for me, and that feels better than trusting. But control can also cause me to hurt and disregard others and make poor choices. Control assumes that I know best, but what God whispers (or sometimes hollers) is a knowing of a different kind.

"Be still and know," he says.

Know what?

"Know that *I* am God."

Oh yeah.

So I humble myself and find my rightful place once again.

Relinquishing control reminds us that we're not truly in charge. Letting go of the need for things to go our way allows space for God to have his way in us. Releasing control is just one of many small ways we make room for new growth. Life with God is the very best partnership, and it's one big, amazing lesson in collaborating, considering, and giving up control. This is what leads to real rest.

Do you find yourself being so particular that it gets in the way of loving others? Have you ever recognized in yourself a clingy desire to control? Consider Jesus's kind invitation to learn to take a real rest as he reminds you to be still and know that he is God.

tulips

measuring tapes

$\mathcal{N}\!\!\underline{\underline{o}}\, 7$

MEASURING UP

In the early 1990s, supermodels became a *thing*. Perhaps you remember them: Christy Turlington and her perfectly symmetrical face, Naomi Campbell and her glistening skin, Kate Moss and her waiflike stature, Cindy Crawford and that mole, Nikki and Krissy Taylor and their natural girl-next-door beauty. My middle-school best friend and I studied these undeniably gorgeous young women the same way the rest of our classmates memorized movie stars. We laid on her floor for hours, poring over the newest issues of *Glamour*, *InStyle*, and *Vogue*, each choosing our favorite images to cut out and hang on our bedroom walls. We gave each other makeovers to try the eye lining techniques the makeup artists explained in three-step articles. My friend's hallway became our catwalk, where we practiced our runway walks and perfected our pouty, model faces.

By my fifteenth birthday, fashion magazine tear-outs covered the walls of my bedroom. I noted the poses, the styles, the hair and makeup, the smiles. I didn't necessarily want to be one of my super-model idols; I just secretly wondered how I stacked up. If this was the standard of beauty, where did I fit in the hierarchy?

Gradually, the fixation that started innocently enough wormed its way into my adolescent heart and began to leave a mark. The magazines started to lose their appeal. I never felt pretty enough or skinny enough or fashionable enough, and I had had enough. No matter how hard I tried, my skin would always be pale, my lips would always be thin, and my measurements would never measure up (or down) to those of the supermodels plastered above my bed. So in a flash of inspired insight, I took the pictures off my wall, tossed them into the recycle bin, and vowed to never again read a fashion magazine. That was more than 25 years ago, and I've made good on the promise.

A decade and a half later, Instagram entered the picture.

I traded the casual one-finger turn of a glossy page for the convenient thumb scroll of the screen. It was entertaining to witness the behind-the-scenes images posted by friends and strangers, and it was a part of my online business, so it felt necessary. Slowly, though, as the photos became more polished and my heart became more discontented and unsettled, I fell right back into my teenage temptation to use comparison to measure my worth.

Her kitchen is so gorgeous; ours is dark and the counters are dated. She's better than me.

Her style is strange; mine is so classic. I'm better than her.

I can't see any cellulite on her; my thighs are so dimply. I need to cover up and work harder.

They always take the most luxurious vacations; I wish we could afford that.

On and on it went until the comparison and conclusion-drawing became second nature, humming along in the background of my heart, yanking my sense of worth to and fro and destining me for the worst case of self-esteem whiplash. *I'm enough! I'm not. I'm enough! I'm not.*

I knew once again that I needed to eliminate this stumbling block. With the click of the Unfollow button, I removed accounts whose photos made me judge myself or others or whose follower numbers stirred up envy. Anything that caused me to linger and assess whether or not I measure up was cleared from my feed. It eased my comparison hangover—at first.

There's some wisdom to my actions. If anything

causes us to repeatedly stumble in our hearts or minds, it makes sense to knock it out of the way. But as I began to realize, the simple choice to avoid a magazine or unfollow on social media only scratches the surface of the real issue. Even when I shunned images of the unattainable beauty of a supermodel or the highlight reel of an influencer, I found plenty of other places to compare: women at church or at the grocery store, even my own friends. I had more wisdom to gain.

• • ▪ • •

Our oldest son, Ethan, runs cross-country for his high school. He is fast, trains hard, and is eager to improve. One evening, Ryan, Audrey

running shoes

(our youngest), and I went together to watch Ethan race. It was a twilight run, starting at eight under the lights of an old high school field. Music blared and runners stretched and did warm-up laps around the track. The bleachers were peppered with parents in their down-filled puffer coats, holding umbrellas in case the clouds opened up.

We caught up with Ethan before the race, patting him on the back. "Stay focused. Run hard. This is your race!"

The crowd of boys in their various school colors huddled together at the starting line, and the gun sounded. Off they went, with Ethan in the front of the pack. On the first of eight laps, he came around the curve to where we were cheering from the stands, looked up at us, and gave us a thumbs-up.

Adorable and heart swelling for a mom? Absolutely. *Man, he's such a good kid*, I thought. *I'm so glad he still likes us.* It reminded me of when he was a preschooler playing indoor soccer for the first time. None of the boys knew what they were doing; they ran in a little mob in their striped soccer socks and parks-and-rec T-shirts, chasing the ball and scanning the sidelines for their parents.

It was sweet that Ethan looked up at us during his race. He wanted us to see him, to cheer for him. He wanted to impress us with his running, his determination, his attitude. On the second lap, he did the same, taking the final curve and turning his face to us, smiling.

By the third and fourth laps, he was losing his place at the front, yet he was still giving us a quick arm pump as he passed by. At that point, Ryan and I glanced at each other and agreed, "He needs to stop looking around and just run his race." As he came around the corner, we both yell-cheered, "Stay focused. Run hard. This is your race!" On his final lap, he didn't look at us but instead peered behind him to gauge his competition, finally sprinting with the last of his energy to the finish. He had a fine race, finishing in the middle of the pack and improving on his personal record by a second or two, but he knew he could do better. All that effort spent looking around had cost him his chance to run his best race.

When Ethan first told me he wanted to run cross country, I was supportive but a little confused. "You know it's a lot of running, right?" I'm not a runner. My lungs and shins don't like it, and speed has never been my thing. The running metaphors in the Bible are a bit lost on me because of my lack of interest in the sport. The ones about salt and yeast, sure—I like to bake. But running, not so much. However, after watching Ethan run his first race, I could see what the famous *run your race* Scripture was talking about: "Let us run with endurance the race that lies before us, keeping our eyes on Jesus, the source and perfecter of our faith" (Hebrews 12:1-2 HCSB).

AWARDS

trophy

medal

ribbon

Diverting my eyes from the things that caused me to compare did not make the problem of soul-deep unrest and uncertainty about my value go away. The supermodels with their flawless faces were not the problem; Instagram with its endless images of perfect houses, trendy outfits, and polished smiles was not either. My instinct to compare revealed a part of my troubled, tired heart: I was looking for my sense of value and identity in places it would never be found. I used comparison to help me figure out who I was, how I stacked up, and whether I was more or less beautiful/creative/skinny/successful, and then I drew conclusions about my worth based on my assessment.

The problem with comparison is that it leads my eyes away from the purposed path ahead. I'm like my adorable Ethan running his race: good-intentioned but distracted, eyes darting and losing focus. I was earnestly running the race of life trying to meet my own impossible expectations, unaware of how I constantly looked up into the stands, concerned with who was watching, how I looked, whether I was doing it right, who was in front of me, and who was behind, all the while tripping up and missing the point.

The real rest Jesus invites us to experience is more than the mid-race, hands-on-knees breather we think we need. It's so much more. It's a chance to lay down the behaviors and the beliefs that are keeping us frantic and trade them in for real purpose, belonging, identity, and

let us run
with endurance
the race that lies
before us,

keeping our eyes on Jesus,
the source and perfecter
of our faith.

HEBREWS 12:1-2 HCSB

love. Insecurity is a sneaky beast, ravenous and unassuming. It twists truths and tells us lies about who we are. It keeps us bound and striving, preoccupied with self and trying so hard to prove we're valuable that we miss the real truth.

No amount of striving, proving, performing, or hiding will make us more acceptable. No one in the stands can give us enough validation. No race ranking will make us worthier. Comparing ourselves to those with less is just as damaging as measuring ourselves up against those with more. The woman with the perfect manicure and the dream job and the one with the messy topknot who still hasn't figured out what she wants to be when she grows up are each equally beloved because of Christ.

His final words on the cross made it known; we have nothing left to do and no one else to be to earn God's favor. *It is finished*. He calls me enough. He calls you enough.

● ● ◗ ● ◗

After a lifetime of running hard for approval, feeling vaguely discontent with a side of frantic, and constantly trying to see if I measured up, Jesus's invitation to slow down and focus on him was as enticing as ever. There's a better way to live—free of comparison and chasing after what isn't meant to be ours—and it all comes down to where we focus our eyes and our hearts while we run.

If you train your gaze up ahead, you'll see Jesus at the finish line, waving his arms to grab your attention: *I'm up here. I've already won. Keep your beautiful feet moving toward me. Don't worry about who's watching or how you're doing. Stay focused. Run hard. This is your race.*

flag banner

Airstream

№ 8

DON'T FORGET TO BREATHE

For most of his adult life, Ryan dreamed of traveling around the country road-trip style with our family. When he brought it up every now and then, the idea was usually met with a *That sounds unrealistic* sort of response from normal, dream-killing old me. Taking a big trip sounded exciting but highly unconventional, and it would disrupt our lives. Embracing change is not my gift. It felt like one of those items you put on a bucket list but never actually get to or maybe what a more adventurous, less conventional family might do. We were not wanderlusts; we were a family firmly planted, with jobs and school and a mortgage and a dog.

And then one day, I shocked Ryan and myself (and anyone who knew me) and said yes. *Yes, let's take our family on that trip around the country.*

It took us a year of planning, and on the last day of April, the six of us loaded the car, waved good-bye to our friends, and pulled out of our neighborhood with a gleaming silver Airstream trailing behind us. In it we had packed all the necessities for four months of traveling: just enough clothes, only the cooking essentials, linens to transform the couch and dinette into beds each night, a small stack of games, a ziplock baggie of Legos for the kids, way more camera equipment than needed, and our computers so we could work remotely.

My blog and online business were doing well enough to support our family, and since Ryan was already a vital part of the business, he retired early from his firefighting career to work full-time with me. We thought the public school would have a laundry list of requirements for the kids, but pulling them out two months early was as easy as simply signing a piece of paper. We even staged our home and had real estate photos taken just in case we got the urge to sell while on the open road. Ryan's lifelong dream and my finally saying yes changed the course of our lives.

• • • • •

Before I said yes to this adventure, I was waking up to the reality that my efforts to control my life and prove my worth were not working. Ryan and I recognized that our family was on a similarly dangerous path. We were tangled up in the worries and seemingly innocuous pursuits of the world, mightily distracted and hurried and busy. It wasn't all bad. We were generous with our home, always hosting and inviting and including others. Our kids grew, as did our neighborhood friendships, and soon our days were filled with playdates, ringing doorbells, multiple pairs of Velcro Nikes strewn across the entry floor, and the constant whiz of Nerf bullets through the hall. These were good years, and we were grateful to do them in community.

In the midst of the neighborhood gatherings and group vacations and quiet family walks that inevitably grew into noisy multifamily walks, Ryan and I looked at each other with a vague sense that something was off. Our lives were so full and busy and loud and fast that we never stopped to intentionally decide if this was the life we wanted, the life God wanted for us. Were we loving and serving our family well? The truth was, the stretch of years that included getting married, buying and updating a house, having four kids, and diving headfirst into the American dream were so full and went so quickly, we didn't really know who we were or if we liked who we were becoming. We needed a reset.

• • • • •

At the end of my Tuesday barre class (a ballet-inspired workout using small movements to increase strength and flexibility), we finish with

And my God
will meet all your needs
according to the riches
of his glory
in Christ Jesus.

PHILIPPIANS 4:19 NIV

a two-minute plank. My fellow classmates and I have already spent 50 minutes exhausting our muscles with small down-an-inch, up-an-inch movements, so our bodies are warm, our heart rates are up, and muscles are shaky. The final plank is like the cherry on the top of our workout—the grueling finishing touch. We begin on our mats on all fours, hands lined up directly under our shoulders and knees under our hips. Then we stretch our legs out behind us, knees hovering, toes on the floor, backs straight, abs pulled in. Then we stay there. For two, long minutes. It doesn't sound that hard, but halfway in, my body is usually trembling.

Our instructor watches the clock and shouts encouragements over the music: "You've got this!" and "You're stronger than you think!" and "Don't forget to breathe!" That last reminder might seem unnecessary, but without fail, her words shake us all to an awareness. We're so focused on getting through the physical challenge that we catch ourselves holding our breath. Her specific instruction to breathe in through the nose and out through the mouth isn't only about the taking in of oxygen. It's also a reminder to check in with our bodies and pay attention to our form. We make adjustments and slow our breath and plank our way through the final minute with greater intention, motivated to finish well.

The around-the-country journey was our family's midlife reminder:

Don't forget to breathe! God wanted so much more for each of us, and we needed the time to step back, slow down, pause the distractions, and reconnect to discover what that was. I know not every family can take a four-month-long deep breath, but that's what reshaped our family.

● ◆ ▶ ● ◆

On the 15,500-mile, 107-day road trip, we traveled counterclockwise around the country, mostly sticking to the perimeter with a few detours inland to hit Kentucky, Nashville, and St. Louis. We hiked through the Redwoods, walked from Times Square to Central Park, stood in awe at the Lincoln Memorial, watched fireworks from George Washington's estate, and took in the pinks and purples and dusty oranges of the Grand Canyon from high above in a helicopter. The kids earned Junior Ranger badges at as many National Parks as we could fit in. We dined at local restaurants, trying chicken and waffles in Savannah, fry bread in New Mexico, and boiled peanuts in South Carolina. We saw black bear, elk, buffalo, and flamingos and had to stay out of the Gulf of Mexico for something called sea lice (ewww).

With no one else to play with, the kids turned to each other. We met up with a few friends around the country, but for the most part,

water bottle

camera

snacks

blanket

first aid kit

the siblings were each other's playmates. As a family, we had time for meaningful conversations and simple forms of entertainment: reading, drawing, playing with dice, and carving sticks with pocketknives. It's crazy how many toys we left behind and how unmissed they were. Because we were living in less than 300 square feet, we didn't buy souvenirs, and it took all the pressure off when the kids asked. *Sorry, Audrey. Yes, it is adorable, but we just don't have room for a life-sized stuffed buffalo from Yellowstone or a bucket of seashells from the beach.* They each had one small bin of clothes that were worn in different combinations over and over again. Our limited wardrobes made doing laundry in the coin-operated machines at campgrounds surprisingly easy.

Ryan and I worked a little from the road to maintain our businesses and to share about the trip in real time on social media and my blog. We got everything necessary done in a fraction of the time, which made us question the many hours we committed to work when at home. All pressure was off to cook elaborate meals, since all I had were two small burners, one wooden spoon, and about 24 inches of counter space. A tiny door separated our bedroom from the rest of the trailer, but with nowhere to go, no TV, and spotty internet, we ended up adopting the same sleep schedule as the kids.

Ethan grew from a boy to a young man right before our eyes during those four months. Each night before we tucked him into his dinette-turned-bed, he asked deep faith questions. The conversations that followed were mostly lost on the younger kids, but I can't help but imagine that their big brother's questions and Ryan and me engaging with him as he wrestled with them set the tone for a new way of being in our family. Ethan grew emotionally, spiritually, and physically, and none of it was lost on us. That would not have been the case if we were back home, surrounded by friends, distracted with normal life, and without the routine of spending all day together.

Brady, our second child, was curious and engaged everywhere we went. He was the first to ask a question of a tour guide or ranger, often the only kid in a tour group of mostly adults to show such interest. His natural inquisitiveness and thoughtfulness were on full display, and for the first time, I wasn't too busy to see it.

History came alive for Mason as we stood where Martin Luther King Jr. delivered his "I Have a Dream" speech or walked the battlefield at Gettysburg. He surprised us with his preference for the big cities and the most famous of sites. We worry sometimes whether he feels lost among the four kids because he's the most

Yosemite National Park

introverted and least expressive. On this trip, we made extra efforts to make him feel special, seen, and important. In return, he was quick to hold our hands and request a seat at the table next to us. His little heart needed us to be present, and we were.

Audrey had just turned six years old and walked miles each day. Miles! And with hardly a complaint. She kept up with her big brothers, she was pushed in her food preferences, she listened to books in the car beyond her kindergarten interests, and she kept her sweet smile and adorable sense of humor the whole time. What an enormous privilege as parents to have had these moments with our kids.

For Ryan and me, the break from normal life gave us time and space to talk and dream and begin the tender process of exposing long-neglected issues. We learned that we're not good at making quick decisions, and we had to make a million adjustments on the fly to figure it out. The long hours spent together in the car forced us to find more to talk about than the next day's schedule and cute things the kids said. This intimate, honest, nowhere-to-hide way of living wasn't always easy. But it drew us closer and gave us a chance to take a breath and consider what adjustments to make once the trip was over.

The road trip slowed us down. It halted our regular routines and showed us just how unnecessarily busy we had become. The distractions we had just accepted as normal were yanking our attention all over the place, never allowing us to be fully present. They were robbing us of joy and contentment. They kept our relationships shallow and us striving. We didn't want to continue living like that.

• • • • •

When Jesus invites us to take a rest, there are costs. We have to lay a few things down in order to posture our hearts to receive the benefits. Accepting the invitation might require us to look closely at our lives to remove unnecessary activities, alter habits, and eliminate excess.

What routines are wearing you out? Have you adopted routines that keep you from fully engaging with the people around you? In what practical, everyday ways can you intentionally choose to slow down, scale back, and live unhurried?

These are good, purposeful questions to ponder. However, it's important not to stop there. There's a deeper reason we choose lives of hustle and distraction. We do it to ourselves. Sometimes it's unconscious, and we're just going along with what everyone else does. Our Western culture encourages us to squeeze every ounce of productivity, entertainment, and superficial pleasure out of our days, and it's easy to get sucked in.

But at a deeper level, I wonder if we choose to be busy because it serves us in some way. Having a lot to do makes us feel important and necessary, and we like feeling that way. Staying busy is a way to hide from hurt and to keep lingering shame covered up, and that seems like a much better option than facing those things head-on. Maybe it feels safer to remain on the surface and not fully engage with life and relationships for fear that any real examination will leave us exposed, vulnerable, lacking. When we have little to distract us, our true selves are on display, and when we don't know who we are or if we like who we're becoming, it feels terrifying.

Are you busy and distracted? Do you avoid a break from your routine out of fear that you'll discover uncomfortable truths? Have you forgotten to breathe? Jesus extends an invitation into real rest, and you need not be timid to accept it. As you slow your pace and release your addiction to hurry, hustle, and distraction, he is faithful to shine light into the dark places of your heart in order to bring about true freedom and transformation. Releasing the addiction to busyness leads to an abundant life of peace.

rain coat

$\mathcal{N}^{\underline{o}}$ 9

AT THE END OF THE COMFORT ZONE

Vivian, my best friend's mom, is a spunky, faithful, small but mighty woman with endless energy. She left her Midwestern life at age 20 to see what Arizona had to offer and has been there ever since. On her first date with her now husband, she wore white jeans to a mud-slinging monster truck rally just for laughs. Late at night, she sneaks onto the golf course behind their house with her grandkids to run through the sprinklers. She started a Bible study for the white-haired, snowbird, golf-club ladies just to see who would come, and 20 years later, it's still going strong. Her name means *full of life*, and she truly is as vivacious as they come.

On the entry table of her desert home is a well-worn Bible, and on top is a small porcelain tile engraved with Vivian's favorite saying: *Life begins at the end of your comfort zone.*

She's been saying it for years and lives like it's true. Honestly, it never resonated with me. The way I've always seen it, at the end of our comfort zone is…discomfort. I much prefer comfort to adventure. I've never been an adrenaline junky or one who welcomes risk. Give me the choice of learning to surf or pleasantly watching from the shore, and I'll choose a towel in the sand every single time. I cried on the first day of school every year, not in anticipation of missing my mom, but because new things make me nervous. I like words like "routine," "familiar," "known." If you push me to where I have no control, where trust is the only posture to have, where I am not sure if I'll succeed or fail, where I have the potential to disappoint someone, *anyone*—oh, man, get me out of there! And fast.

● ● ● ● ● ●

During our family's big road trip, we spent a few days exploring Yosemite National Park, one of Ryan's favorite places. We arrived at the right time of year for warm spring weather and plenty of snowmelt to keep the waterfalls bursting. One afternoon, we took a hike along a path that led to a series of falls. After making it to the first one, we found a place off the path and under the shade of trees with large, flat boulders to picnic on. We watched the other hikers going up and down the trail, noticing the very wet attire of those returning from

backpack

the top. The larger waterfall up ahead was pushing over a spectacu-
lar amount of water, and the overspray was drenching the onlookers.
Ryan couldn't wait for us to go see it for ourselves.

I'm not a super-high-maintenance girl. Don't forget that we were
living in a tiny trailer with zero closet space and barely enough room for
the minimal makeup I brought along for months on end. But I didn't
want to get my hair and clothes all wet. I wasn't wearing a rain jacket
and wasn't all that excited about walking back down the trail in wet

shoes. My naturally thick and somewhat frizz-prone hair takes forever to do, and I had just washed and dried and styled it that morning and was looking forward to a few days of not having to worry about it. The allure of seeing the waterfall up close just wasn't enough to compel me out of my comfort zone. "Go on ahead," I said. "I'll wait here."

Ryan was slightly annoyed. "Seriously? You're going to miss seeing one of the world's most breathtaking waterfalls that is only a few steps away because you don't want to get your hair wet? This is a chance for a memory!" It was important to him that we go as a family. I didn't want to spoil the day, so I got over myself and my nice, smooth hair. I put on Ryan's raincoat, wrapping the hood tightly around my face like a true waterfall lightweight and walked with the kids up the remaining steps of the slippery trail.

The view was amazing, and the water rushed with such uncontainable power, I was in a state of awe. The roar made it nearly impossible to hear each other, which made us laugh. It was very wet, but thanks to my fashionable hood choice, my hair remained protected. I snapped a few pictures, and then we walked back down and went on our way.

It *was* really cool. Yet...

I wish I could tell you that I was changed by that experience and motivated—even elated!—to take new risks. But I was unchanged. It was a waterfall. It got me wet. It was fine. It was fun even. My hair was covered, my shorts dried quickly, and I'm glad for Ryan's sake that I followed him up the trail. But truthfully, I would've been perfectly content never having seen it.

I know that sounds terrible. And so old-ladyish. Why am I like this?

My instinct is to crave sameness, convention, the expected and known. I just adore feeling secure and comfortable. When I dig down into my desire for what's comfortable, I find that it is less about the warm, cozy feelings it offers and more about the anxiety-inducing uncertainty it avoids. Boundaries are created, and I call them comfort zones, but the truth is they are more like thick imaginary walls protecting me from what could invade my status quo and blocking me from stepping into new experiences.

● ◆ ◗ ◆ ◆

I'm reminded of the story of the Exodus in the Bible. Moses had just done the whole ten plagues thing, and Pharaoh finally agreed to let the people go. But then he changed his mind and had the Israelites cornered by the

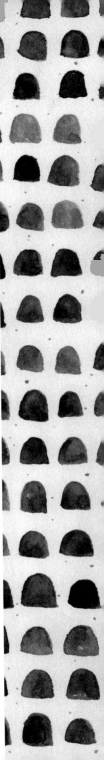

overpowering Egyptian army on one side and the great Red Sea on the other. Just when the Israelites thought they would surely die, God opened up a dry path through the middle of the sea, with walls of salt water with fish and whales on either side, like the glass-walled underground aquarium not too far from our house. When the Egyptians saw what was happening, they rushed to follow with chariots and horses and feather-plumed helmets. You may know how the story ends: The Israelites make it to the other side, but the waves crash down violently upon Pharaoh's army, and they are swallowed whole. A win for God and the Israelites; a bad day for ancient Egypt.

Can you imagine what this must have been like? To know for sure you had no way to escape, yet through an unimaginable miracle, you do? The rescued Israelites sing a song of thanks and praise to God for an entire chapter. But it's what happens next that is surprising. They grumble. It turns out the desert they have escaped to is not flowing with milk and honey (that would come later, in the Promised Land), and they are thirsty and hungry. *This is terrible!* they shout. *Remember back in Egypt, when we had all the meat and bread we wanted? We wish we were back home, where things were normal and familiar and at least we had good food to eat. It would have been better for us to die at home full than here, where we're hungry!* But they forgot one tiny detail: Back home in Egypt, they were slaves (Exodus 16:1-3).

As silly as it sounds, I empathize with the Israelites. I felt like that too when I was waking up to the un-fineness of my life. *Take me back, Lord, to when things were normal and familiar, before I became aware of how tangled up in self-imposed insecurity I have become. It was cozy and comfortable there.* But back where it was normal and familiar, I was a slave. The way I was living life, with my striving and my endless pursuit of proving myself worthy, of doing all I could to keep things fine and comfortable...well, it had me dangerously bound up. That's what a comfort zone is, after all. It's one big, innocent-looking lie that tries to fool you into thinking you should stay right there in the middle of it. In reality, the comfort zones we create for ourselves are the exact things that keep us from truly living.

● ● ● ● ●

When the kids were little, we took daily walks to the neighborhood park, stopping every three steps to pick up a new treasure—a pinecone, a rock, a dandelion plucked from the crack of the sidewalk. "Mommy, is this alive?" they would ask. And like the good child-development student I was, my answer always bounced back as a question, "You tell me! Does it grow?" Perhaps that's a simplified definition of what being alive means, but in general, it works. Does a rock grow? No, not

THINGS TO COLLECT ON A WALK

acorn

buttercup

pinecone

leaves

alive. Does a buttercup grow? Yes, alive. Does a stick grow? Nope, not alive. Does a branch grow? Yep, alive.

Our comfort zones are typically designed to keep us bubble-wrapped, protected, and ignorantly numbed and distracted to avoid discomfort so we can pretend we're living.

But do we grow? No.

So even my kids can tell us, that's not being alive.

I returned from the road trip aware that I needed to rediscover my identity. I was ashamed of the ways I had put on my self-protective armor and the inadvertent damage those choices caused. My hands were open wide, palms up, as vulnerable and fragile as ever, but this time I was ready and desperate for healing. I wanted to grow. I wanted to be alive.

I hoped beyond hope that Vivian was right—that true, *abundant* life would begin as I stepped cautiously out of my comfort zone. I hoped that by releasing my grip on the familiar comforts of our life, a space would crack open in my heart to allow me to begin exploring the layers upon layers just waiting to be uncovered.

I was done trying to live my life staying comfortably dry. I didn't even want to stand back anymore with a hood tied tight around my chin, squinting at the overspray. I had a sense that God was inviting me to go stand right under the waterfall, letting his powerful grace, love, and freedom generously pour over me, pounding off the hurts, chiseling away the insecurities. It would be hard and uncomfortable, for sure. But I knew deep down that the only way to initiate true growth (and therefore *life*) was to release my insatiable desire for comfort, to keep my hands open to receive Truth, to learn to trust, to let the living water gently break and heal and smooth and revive. *I'm done with slavery. Lord, set me free.*

The desire for comfort is normal and not always wrong, but when that pursuit holds you back, keeps you numb and disengaged, well, then, maybe the compulsion for comfort has control over you. Are you feeling that? Are you holding so tightly to comforts that you're missing out on truly living? As you accept the invitation to experience the real rest Jesus offers, trust that it goes far beyond the limited view of a cozy couch, fuzzy slippers, and artisan chocolate. And as you peer into your heart to understand why the desire for comfort is so strong, may you be brave enough to release your grip on false security and trust that life and freedom begin at the end of your comfort zone.

Therefore,
if anyone is in Christ,
he is a new creation.
The old has passed away;
behold, the new has come.

2 CORINTHIANS 5:17 ESV

journal + pencil

№ 10

GRABBING THE LIFE PRESERVER

You know that hypothetical question: If your house caught on fire, what would you grab on your way out? The generations before us would undoubtedly answer "photo albums" because those were irreplaceable. Now that most of our photos are stored in an invisible cloud (I still can't quite wrap my mind around that), we can be a bit more creative with our answers. What would you save? For me, it would be the stack of journals I keep on a shelf in my office.

I started journaling at a young age. Unlike my extroverted sisters, who process best through talking and activity, I'm an introvert who needs quiet time alone to make sense of life. My best processing is done with me, my thoughts, an unlined notebook, and a pencil. The diaries of my youth are filled with records of what I did that day, who had a crush on who, the day-to-day drama of being 10 or 14 or 19. I'm an expert notetaker, so most of the journals from my young adulthood are filled with notes from sermons and blogging conferences with an occasional grocery list mixed in. I just found a box of old notebooks, and some of my favorites are the ones with pages of scribbles and doodles made by toddler versions of Mason and Audrey when they just needed some distraction. This ragged collection of my life documented on floral, striped, and linen-covered journals is my most prized possession.

• ◆ ▸ ◆ ◀

During the season when I became more aware of how burdened I was by my attempts to prove my worth, my journals became canvases for my prayers—private conversations with God, my most honest thoughts, a place to ask questions and maybe get answers, but usually not. I was weary and longing for real rest, and journaling was a daily discipline that helped me process my thoughts. That's what I found myself doing one morning at Starbucks in a tiny, tucked away booth with an open notebook and desperate soul.

I had my decaf Americano and probably a slice of pumpkin loaf beside me (because I love Starbucks' pumpkin loaf) as my pencil point met the page and began to reveal what my heart was feeling. The words flowed out in my scribbly half-cursive penmanship as fast as my mind could form them.

I am so burdened by expectations, I wrote. *Self-imposed. Constant. Drowning. Deflating. Sinking.* I lifted my right hand and pressed it against my chest. This was becoming a regular thing: An invisible lump sat right under the surface and just wouldn't go away, and applying pressure with my open hand seemed to help. And then, like a movie, a scene played itself out in my mind, and my pencil moved quickly to capture it in my journal.

decaf Americano

I'm paddling and paddling, trying to stay afloat. "I'm fine!" I say as I keep my head above water, smiling. But behind the smiling face, I am terrified. Under water and deep in my soul, it is dark, inky blue. I am faking it and getting so tired. My legs churn, treading water frantically. Jesus is there next to me, watching. Maybe he's in a boat? Maybe he's standing right on top of the water? I can't tell. He's waiting patiently, a white life ring held casually in the crook of his arm, the kind that hangs from a lifeguard tower. Reminding me, calling out to me. "I'm right here," he says. "Grab hold," he says. "I'm fine!" I reply. "I'm fine. I'm so glad you're right there, Jesus. It is so good to know you are close. I see you. I trust you. I believe in you."

And this is where it got strange. I felt as though my pencil was no longer controlled by me but by the Holy Spirit within me.

But do you depend on me? I wrote, as if God himself was speaking. *Or do you just keep doing your own thing?*

I closed my eyes to catch my breath. Took a sip of my drink. Then went back to the page.

I will give you rest, he continued. *I will tell you who I am. Shhh.*

And that was it: The picture of the water, the life preserver, and a struggling me disappeared. I closed my journal and carried on with my day, subtly aware that what happened in the notebook and within my spirit that morning was pivotal. Later that night when I looked back over what I had written in the coffee shop, I thought for sure I would find the words, *I will tell you who you are.* That's what I've always been after. *Please tell me who I am, Lord!* But instead, I found the answer I didn't know I needed.

I will tell you who I am.

I wanted it to be about me, but instead, it was about him.

I knew a lot about God. I believed wholeheartedly in him. I was doing a lot for him. But maybe he was right when he wrote those questions in my notebook that day. Maybe I was depending on my own ways, my own ability and effort, more than I was trusting in his. It's not like I was denying him; I believed in him and knew he was always near. I could imagine him right beside me as I did my thing. However, my lips formed a smile as if all was well—while the rest of me sank and grew weary from trying to stay afloat and present an "everything's fine" exterior. I thought I was capable, but the truth was, reliance on my own vision of life was drowning me.

● ● ● ● ●

When the kids were little, they took swimming lessons from Miss Jody. She was a schoolteacher during the year and used her backyard pool for swimming lessons every summer. She was friendly, great with kids, and a competent swimmer, and she totally looked the part with her water shoes, full-sleeve swimsuit, nose with white zinc, and faded hat. When it came time for the kids to put their faces in the water or leave the comfort of the shallow end, she was no-nonsense. Her job was to teach these little ones how to swim, and she was determined to do it in two weeks of lessons.

The class always included a few water-timid kids, the ones who barely dipped their chins in the water and gripped Miss Jody tightly if she pulled them from their spot on the stairs. When they tried to float, they could never relax, and you can't float if your arms and legs are flailing about. When they attempted to swim without putting their faces in the water, their little bottoms sunk, and they resorted to the doggy paddle—not what Miss Jody had in mind for her students.

The new swimmers were anxious and didn't yet trust their instructor. They weren't sure if she was telling them the truth when she said she'd keep them safe and that her way of floating and swimming was better than their more comfortable methods. Trust-building takes time and requires genuinely getting to know the one you're putting your trust in. Without fail, Miss Jody proved herself reliable. My

SWIMSUITS

one-piece

wrap

bikini

halter

Let us hold unswervingly
to the hope we profess,
for he who promised
is faithful.

HEBREWS 10:23 NIV

water-loving kids took lessons with her for six consecutive summers, and I was amazed every time that by the end of the session, the once fraidy-cat swimmers in the classes bravely crawl-stroked and side-breathed their way across the pool. In just two weeks, they learned to relax, to let go of their quick, flappy strokes and the instinct to keep their heads above the water.

· · · · ·

Sometimes it just feels easier to trust in ourselves, to rely on our own ability, effort, and vision for how things should go, doesn't it? Even if it's not quite as fruitful, self-reliance is much less risky. We can be just like those kiddos in the pool; our ability is limited, our knowledge incomplete, our energy wasted with our flailing efforts. All the while, a strong, well-intentioned teacher stands at our side, seeing the full picture and offering to show us how best to live. If only we'd just stop all the unnecessary striving.

I was shaken by the picture God gave me in my journal of me treading water and refusing his help. As much as I truly believed in the person of God, it was clear: I didn't trust that his way was better than mine. My heart was divided between faith in Jesus and faith in myself, and the indecision was not working out in my favor. His offer for real rest was exactly what I needed, and that morning in Starbucks made it very obvious that the only thing stopping me from rest was my own stubborn self-reliance. His invitation was right there. *Grab hold! I'm right here. I'll rescue you!*

What stops me from surrendering my own ideas and plans and ways in favor of God's? What keeps me treading water and striving for love, belonging, and identity instead of accepting his invitation for absolute healing? It all comes down to trust.

Trust requires submission and the belief that the one you're putting your trust in has your best interests in mind. It's easy to trust when the stakes are low. I trust that my dentist is going to clean my teeth properly even though I don't know exactly what he's doing. I trust that my son will learn algebra when he goes to math class (Lord, bless all middle-school teachers). I trust that the Uber driver will take the fastest route and that the barista will use decaf espresso instead of regular. I partially trust all day, every day in a million different ways. But when the stakes are high and it's a matter of my identity or my deepest needs and most vulnerable fears, that's when trust gets hard.

To release control, to give up comfort, to deliberately eliminate busyness, to train our eyes away from comparison, to finally see the weeds that are tripping us up and choking us out, and to begin the work of pulling them out requires *complete* trust. Before we can fully trust, we need to get to know the One in whom we're placing our trust. When all I wanted was to hear Jesus tell me who I am, instead he invited me into real rest with the promise of telling me who *he* is. He invites you into the same.

Cautiously, eyes locked on his, we reach out our hands and grab hold of the outstretched life preserver. *Lord, we're listening. Tell us who you are.*

life preserver

PART THREE

WE'RE INVITED
TO LEARN THE UNFORCED
RHYTHMS OF GRACE

popcorn

№. 11

PAY ATTENTION TO SEE

The movie theater in our town started showing films in 3D, and the kids were excited. We bought tickets; loaded up on an extra-large bucket of popcorn, Junior Mints (for me), and Skittles (for them); put on our special black plastic glasses; and settled in to be swept up in a delightfully fictitious story. To watch a favorite character on the big screen is one thing, but to feel like you are right in the middle of the scene, as if you might actually touch those make-believe things with your own hands, takes movie-watching to a whole new level. Well, at least it does if the 3D glasses work with your eyes.

I was born with an eye condition called strabismus, also known as "lazy eye." Yep, I'm one of those people with an eye that wanders and makes you feel weird when you're having a face-to-face conversation because you don't know which eye to focus on. To be fair, my eyes are not that bad, but only because I've had three eye surgeries. With each surgery—at ages 3, 10, and 18—the doctor cut a tiny piece of the muscle in my left eye and pulled it just a touch tighter to aesthetically align my eyes.

Lining up my eyes was one part of the solution. The other, arguably bigger issue is getting my eyes to work together. My right eye is dominant and my go-to for focusing; the left one tends to let the right eye do all the work. This means I don't naturally use both eyes equally, and therefore I have a harder time with tasks that require eye cooperation, like depth perception. And watching 3D movies.

My vision is just fine, and thankfully the surgery succeeded in lining up my eyes to avoid that "which one do I look at" confusion. Learning to get my eyes to work together is the part that takes regular practice, effort, and attention. As a little girl, I wore glasses with tape on the lens to coax my left eye into fully participating. In old family photos, you might spot a ponytailed redhead with an eyepatch (that's me!), and my mom says we did muscle exercises at bedtime, although I have no recollection of this. She probably made me think the eye-strengthening exercises were just a game, because she's a fun mom like that.

Even now, I have to put conscious effort toward focusing with both eyes. On days when my eyes are especially tired, the left one gets lazy and the overworked right eye begins to ache. Our eyes were made to share the load and work together, and even more, when they function as designed, they enable us to truly see the world around us with depth and fullness and dimension. Mine don't do it automatically, and in some ways, it's a blessing. It acts as a reminder that sometimes you have to pay attention to truly see.

● ● ● ● ●

The first time I met my eventual brother-in-law, we were at a J. Crew store. I was home from college visiting my sister Amy, and she was excited to introduce me to her boyfriend. Shopping felt like a good, low-pressure setting for our first encounter. I remember two things from that day: (1) Eric had frosted tips and wore a puka shell necklace (so very appropriate for this unfortunate fashion era), and (2) he picked up a pair of pants, held them up to me, and said, "These would look great on you." I liked him instantly.

Eric is the smarter, more socially driven, male version of me. He's a feeler and a deep thinker; he works hard and loves his family; he is annoyed at his insecurities

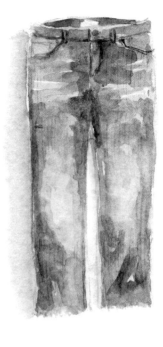

jeans

and not afraid to admit it. This past year, he sought out a counselor to help him sort through some things. When I asked him what compelled his pursuit of help, he said something profound: He realized the last time he made a proactive decision was when he asked Amy to marry him. That was 16 years ago. Everything since then happened quickly—kids, dog, house, job—and he was tired of feeling like a by-stander, watching his life happen to him. Eric doesn't wish the details of his life were different; he wishes he felt like an active participant instead of a reactive one. I can totally relate.

One way or another, we all fall into a rhythm of life. It is not always intentional; in fact, I would guess that most of the time, our way of living and being is completely *un*intentional. We do the things we've always done in the ways our family or community or culture says to do it, rarely questioning and usually allowing the finer details to blur into the background. Slowly adopting patterns and routines until they become second nature seems to work for most of us...at least until it doesn't.

Eric began to notice how he felt unimportant and surprisingly empty in the midst of his wonderful life. The insecurities that bound me floated to the surface and just wouldn't go away. The dull pain in my soul was making itself known. You, my friend, are living your own story, and God will gently uncover the truth of your need for him and a new way of being. Just as my eyes ache when they are not working as intended, our souls ache when they are not *living* as intended. It's wise to pay attention to that ache.

● ◆ ● ● ◆

Jesus has a solution for all of us who wish to live in an easier, lighter, more meaningful, and purposeful way: "Walk with me and work with

Thyme

me," he says. "Watch how I do it. Learn the unforced rhythms of grace. I won't lay anything heavy or ill-fitting on you" (Matthew 11:28-30 MSG).

In more traditional versions of the Bible, this is the part that references a yoke, as in "take my yoke upon you and learn from me" (Matthew 11:29 NIV). A yoke is a wooden beam placed over the shoulders of two animals (like oxen or donkeys) to connect them so they can move in unison as they pull a plow or a cart. At first glance, the metaphor seems odd. *We're talking about rest, Jesus. Why the mention of a tool used for hard, laborious work?* But scooch in a little closer and you'll see what he's getting at: Life requires effort. Jesus never promises a trouble-free, easy-peasy existence. There is beauty and goodness and truth, of course, but also difficulty, sadness, loss, and hardship. We are not made to hide, be numb, and sleepwalk all our days; we are made to be alive, and life requires effort.

How we move through our lives is up to us. We can hit autopilot, allowing life to just happen to us and knock us about like one of those metallic balls in a flashy pinball machine (Eric will tell you this is no way to live). We can move with do-it-yourself determination and look to the world, circumstances, successes, failures, relationships, possessions, and popularity to assign us meaning and value (I'll tell you this is no way to live). Or, as Jesus suggests, we can wake up to the truth, willingly surrender our independent way of life that leads to dissatisfaction and exhaustion, and instead align ourselves with him. Will it still be work? Yes. But when done in connection to him, he promises it will not feel heavy or ill-fitting.

• • • • •

The back door opened, and Mason hurriedly slipped off his backpack, reached in, and pulled out a pink piece of paper. "Will you come to my field trip?" he asked, still out of breath after running home from the bus. I love that my work-from-home schedule allows me to join the kids on field trips, and I try to do it as often as possible. I've been to the pumpkin patch, the Washington State History Museum, the zoo, the wildlife park, a salmon estuary, the art museum, Chinatown, and now, after signing the pink paper in Mason's hands, Camp Seymore for a fifth-grade camp.

On the day of the much-anticipated field trip, we broke up into small groups, rotating between four activities led by peppy YMCA camp counselors. The reptile room, with its skeletons, shed skins, live snakes, and lizards, was surprisingly less creepy than I imagined. Archery proved to be an entertaining challenge, with arrows flying wildly and only a select few hitting the targets across the range. Dissecting a squid was just as gooey and fishy smelling as I remembered

WHAT YOU NEED TO TAKE A CANOE RIDE

life jacket

oar

canoe

This is what the Sovereign Lord,
the Holy One of Israel, says:
"Only in returning to me
and resting in me will you be saved;
in quietness and confidence
is your strength."

ISAIAH 30:15 NLT

from my science-class days. But canoeing was my favorite.

The kids partnered up, buckled on their bright-orange life vests, and stepped carefully into the tippy aluminum boats. It was a mild spring day, but even so, the salty Puget Sound water was cold, and not even the bravest of boaters wanted to risk falling in. I stood on the dock with the other parent chaperones and watched with amusement. Some boats hardly moved; others turned in circles. We saw paddlers unknowingly struggle against each other with their off-kilter paddling, making for a wobbly and haphazard ride. And then along came Mason and his canoe partner, Noah. They moved smoothly, swiftly, out to the furthest buoy and back without breaking a sweat. I was proud (*That's my kid!*) and also not surprised. Mason has grown up boating and knows the secret to tandem canoeing: Working together is everything. Someone needs to set a paddling cadence, and as long as you pull in unison, you'll move purposefully through the water.

Jesus has set a cadence and invites us to follow his example for how to live a restful, purposeful, peace-filled life. But how do we do this?

I'm tempted to create a checklist. I like a good checklist. It would be nice to simply pick a formula, check off the boxes, and call that abundant life. But if I did that, I'd be right back where I started—caught up in self-effort, pride, and comparison, trying to earn my worth and wearing myself out with the futility of it. Following Jesus is not about adhering to a set of rules or earning accolades through good behavior. This is precisely the yoke of slavery that he came to free us from (Galatians 5:1)!

Instead, he invites us to walk with him, work with him, and watch how he lives so that our hearts, minds, and souls can be made new. He models prayer, fasting, Scripture reading, celebration, community, sabbath, silence, and solitude (among many others) and urges us to practice them as well. These exercises work to strengthen our minds, hearts, and souls and deepen our love of God.

I have to remind my checklist-loving self that in and of themselves, these spiritual disciplines are not the point. They are good and valuable, for sure, but most importantly, they are a means to an end: transformation and real, lasting, beautiful, soul-deep change. Jesus offers us eternal salvation and the promise that we will live with him forever, but he also set up a way for us to live life abundantly *now*, where insecurity and anxiety are traded for confidence and peace, where we no longer depend on our own futile efforts but instead fall in step with his unending rhythms of grace. By adopting his cadence, something beautiful happens: Our vision of who we are, who God is, and what a truly satisfying life looks like begins to line up with Jesus's vision of these same things.

The ache in my soul that I had ignored for so long was telling me it was time to pay attention. The greatest transformation of my mind, heart, and soul was about to take place, and I was finally ready to receive it.

Is your soul aching? Are you longing for true, lasting change from the inside out? Jesus invites you to learn his unforced rhythms of grace, and when you walk in step with him, you will take on your true identity. The greatest gift you can give yourself is to proactively interrupt your life and make space to breathe, uncover, process, ponder, and find answers.

As we pay attention, we will begin to see.

glasses

birthday hat

№ 12

40 BY 40

For as long as I can remember, I've had a fascination and affection for all things self-reflective. My college degree is in child and family psychology. Personality tests, interpersonal communication, group dynamics, birth order...I like all of it. So when the Enneagram was introduced to me, I was quick to look into it.

The Enneagram (pronounced EH-nee-uh-gram) is a personality classification system that has experienced greater popularity over the past few years. While it is not perfect, the Enneagram offered me a language to identify what I saw in myself but never could have articulated on my own. It looks at not only a person's behavior but also the motivation and core longing underneath. You can take a test to find your type, which is all well and good, but the best way to discover which of the nine numbers is most compatible with your personality is to read and study each type until one emerges that makes you feel like someone just read your most private thoughts. *How did they know this about me?* If you get that reaction, it's probably your number.

Type nine is called the Peacemaker, and nothing could sum up my personality better. I abhor conflict. I can see both sides to almost any argument. I am an expert at listening, and I am extremely empathetic. I am easy to be around and generally go along to get along. If you ask for my opinion, I'll be slow to offer it because I probably haven't decided what I think. If I have, I'll avoid sharing for fear it might cause conflict if it's different from yours. I resist being the one to make decisions, especially if the decision impacts another person or a group; I just can't handle feeling responsible if I make the wrong choice. If Ryan asks where I want to go for dinner, I will almost always answer, "I don't care. You choose," because most of the time, even if I do have a preference, I'd rather someone else choose. I like to think I don't cause trouble and am a pleasant companion.

However, the downside of not taking a side or knowing what I like, dislike, and desire is that I often adopt the cares, likes, and desires of those around me and lose myself. In Enneagram language, I'm a type who easily falls asleep to my true self.

It's no wonder I was wrestling with questions of identity. I fell into a pattern of staying quiet, not forming opinions, doing as expected (or as I imagined was expected), forgetting, and downplaying the unique parts of myself all in the name of keeping the peace. This was partially due to my stubborn longing to gain approval and avoid disappointment, but as I was discovering, my personality also played a part.

In a particularly eye-opening moment, I was asked this simple question: What do you care about? I couldn't find an answer. I literally did not know what I cared about. I tripped over words, my heart racing and my mind drawing a blank until I was able to cobble together something about wanting to be the type of mom that picks my kids up from school on time. Sure, my predriving days were peppered with embarrassing moments when I had to call my mom on the payphone outside the school gym because she had forgotten to pick me up from volleyball practice, and I didn't want to put my own kids through that, but seriously? This was the best I could come up with when asked what I care about?

• • • • •

This strange self-forgetfulness showed up in my life in

UGG boots

the oddest of places—for example, when I needed a new pair of slippers. I had worn my cute blue moccasin-style ones so frequently that the cushy fur on the inside was matted down and the leather strings were beginning to break. Since I work from home and my feet are almost always cold, cozy slippers are a daily must-have. I put them on in the morning, and unless I am forced to wear something more suitable for a public outing, I keep them on until I get in bed at night. My dedication to slipper wearing made it seem quite reasonable to splurge on a pair of UGG boots. I had never owned real ones before.

I was online shopping when Ryan came into my office.

"I'm ordering new slippers. Which do you like best?" I asked him.

Truth be told, he thought they were all ugly. I don't think he's alone in being a male who doesn't get the female infatuation with chunky suede slip-on boots from Australia.

"Okay, well, which ones are the *least* ugly?" I asked him.

He pointed at the low gray boots. I added them to my cart, and a few days later, they showed up on our front porch. I like the gray slippers. I wear them every day, and they serve their purpose well. But do you know what I really wanted? The brown ones. I didn't even realize it until later, but I liked the classic brown. That's what I should have picked.

I didn't know what I liked. I didn't know what I wanted in big or small matters. With each passing day, I felt like I was disappearing. Not in the good, godly, dying-to-self way but in the shrinking, hiding, self-protective way. This counterfeit version of me was not honoring the God who created me, nor was it a truthful way to live with the ones I love most. I was robbing my closest friends and loved ones of the chance to genuinely know me, denying my greatest gifts to the world, and hiding my God-given light under a bucket. It all left me feeling invisible, unseen, unimportant, and insignificant.

Learning to walk with Jesus and adopt his unforced rhythms of grace requires showing up and engaging as your fullest, truest self. I needed to practice this. So I decided to write a list.

• • • • •

I got the idea from my childhood best friend. Her life at age 39 looked different than she dreamed, and God was so kind in prompting her to make a list of things she wanted to do in this final year of her thirties—things that brought peace and hope to her fragile heart. Like her, my life at 39 didn't exactly look as I had imagined. From the outside, sure: married with four kids, healthy, living in a pretty house in a charming town. But on the inside, as you know, my heart and soul were starving for wholeness. I was still struggling to answer that *Who am I?* question, and this practice felt like the right next step on my identity journey. It caused me to slow down and pay attention to the desires, delights, and disciplines that would move me into more intentional actions for the year ahead. Writing my list was a tangible way for me to practice figuring out and stating what I wanted based not on expectations or my unhealthy pattern of performing for approval, but on things that brought joy and gratitude and peace to *me*. So I compiled a list of 40 things to do in my thirty-ninth year and called it my 40 by 40 list.

On my list were things I wanted to do out of sheer enjoyment:

Make sourdough bread. I had never tried keeping sourdough starter alive, and I did pretty well—except for that time when I turned the oven on to preheat it and forgot the starter was in there staying warm. The good news is that baked starter smells just as wonderful as a loaf of bread! The bad news is that was the end of my sourdough-bread-baking days.

Volunteer in the nursery. When my kids were little, I was so grateful for the nursery caregivers who loved, held, and entertained my children during church and Bible study. Switching roles and getting to be the caregiver for a whole new generation of moms and kids is a gift, and I love every second of it.

Wear earrings. I've always been very simple in my jewelry preferences—just my wedding ring and a small necklace with my children's initials—and I felt like I could step up my game by adding earrings to the accessory mix. I ordered a few different styles and just decided to wear them. It worked!

There were things I thought I *should* do:

Whiten my teeth. Get a mammogram. Write one handwritten note per month. Interestingly, I didn't do well at the shoulds.

On the list were relationship goals: *Intentional date with Ethan. Intentional date with Brady. Intentional date with Mason. Intentional date with Audrey.* In my mind, I had grand ideas of going skiing or seeing a Broadway show or staying overnight in a hotel with each of the kids,

hoops

glitter studs

tassel

leather

cubes

and none of this happened. But after the year was up, you know what I realized? I'm a good mom. I love those kids and spend a lot of time with each of them. I talk to them and read to them. I cheer for them from the bleachers and drive them to and from all their activities. My goal is for them to know how important and special each of them is to me, and I realized that it doesn't take an elaborate date to tell them.

Two very intangible but important items were on my list: *Heal my gut* and *Feel good in a swimsuit.* For years I had neglected my physical health, so to finally pay attention to my body was a healthy step toward honoring who God made me to be. It's tempting to separate our spiritual lives from our emotional lives, our physical lives from our intellectual lives. We do this all the time. We pay extra attention to one part of us and ignore the rest. But to experience healing and this new graceful rhythm of life, we need to become whole in body, mind, and spirit.

So I went to the doctor. I received intravenous bags of liquid iron. I took a fistful of supplements each day and followed an elimination diet to try to find the source of my tummy troubles. Additionally, I permitted myself to spend time and money on fitness classes. After a year of paying attention to and caring for my body, my health vastly improved. I still did not have the perfect swimsuit body, but I felt stronger, healthier, and proud of myself.

I had a few big things I didn't get to: *Write a children's book. Write a road trip book. Go to Italy.* Yet simply stating the dreams, writing them down, and giving them attention felt vital to my growth.

There is freedom in uncovering who God made us to be—the big and small desires, gifts, and passions he placed within us—and then making choices in our everyday lives that line up with those things. This 40 by 40 exercise gave me space to practice being me, naming what I enjoyed, releasing what wasn't mine to do, and looking at myself with kindness.

Are you searching for a new rhythm of life full of grace and kindness toward yourself? A good place to start is to pay attention to what makes you come alive and do a little more of it.

Nevertheless,
I will bring health and healing to it;
I will heal my people
and will let them enjoy
abundant peace and security.

JEREMIAH 33:6 NIV

candle

№. 13

HE DOESN'T THROW A STONE

One of the items on my 40 by 40 list was to deepen my study of the Enneagram by meeting with a trained coach. This tool was helping me understand myself as God made me, and I was desperate to continue pulling back layers and being open to healing and understanding. I flipped over my favorite Enneagram book and read that the author not only offered coaching, but she lived in Seattle, just an hour north of me. I scheduled an appointment right away.

My coach, Marilyn, greeted me with a smile. I felt her calming presence immediately. I settled in on her red sofa, she on the chair to the left. As she lit a candle, we closed our eyes and sat quietly. Deep breaths in and out—an act of welcoming the Holy Spirit into our time together. I told her about my journey of identity and the ways her book had offered words of understanding. I wondered if she could help me grow more deeply, find freedom, and uncover the answer to my *Who am I?* question. At the end of our hour together, she surprised me by saying she didn't think I needed Enneagram coaching. Instead, she could see that I was actually looking for spiritual direction.

She told me, "There is a place we go each summer where you can look down and see the river below churning, moving swiftly, violently through the narrow rocks. At the far side, the river spills into a deep pool, turquoise in the center, calm, and pleasant. It's as if you are in the river. It is moving fast; it feels tight and dangerous and painful, but it is purposeful. My job as spiritual director is to help move you from those churning waters of wrestling with questions and into the deep pool of knowing who you are and who God is."

I drove away from her home, still shaking and sweaty because I get that way when I'm nervous. But I was ready. *So ready.* I longed for that deep, nourishing pool.

The job of a spiritual director is different from that of a counselor or pastor. Marilyn's relationship with me became that of a wise listener and curious question-asker as she encouraged me to pay attention to the presence and work of God in my life.

She was helping me see.

Our monthly calls started with the lighting of a candle, a moment of silence, and an acknowledgment that the Holy Spirit was near.

Each time we met, I wasn't sure what I wanted to talk about. I didn't know what God wanted to say to me. Without fail, by the time our hour was up, I had tear-stained cheeks and notes scribbled on scrap paper. Long after each of our phone calls, I would ponder those words of encouragement and pictures of the loving way God looks at me.

One day, about a year into our spiritual direction, Marilyn mentioned a Scripture-reading and journaling practice she was working through herself and thought I might like as a next step. She was right. This intentional daily reading and reflecting through the Gospels changed my life. I can't wait to tell you about it.

● ● ▶ ● ●

I love a good devotional. I have a stack of them in a basket now and an app on my phone that makes daily quiet time very accessible. I wrote a blog post once sharing my favorite morning devotional books, and a comment caught me off guard: "Is this really all we're willing to give Jesus? All we have is just an obligatory five minutes to read and then just move on with our day?" That statement could have come off as very critical, and I could have responded defensively: *I'm a busy mom. Five minutes is better than none!* But instead, it convicted me. Daily devotion books have their place and can be priceless resources with their quick readings of Scripture and truth and application, but was that all I was willing to give? And was my current use of those resources growing my knowledge and trust in who God is and who I am and how I should live in this world?

These questions were on my heart at the same time I was seeing Marilyn. My desire to grow and learn was at an all-time high, and I responded by drinking in as much content as I could find. My nightstand was piled with books about identity, emotional health, personality, finding freedom, healthy rhythms, understanding God. I popped earbuds in while I cooked dinner or vacuumed floors or had a moment to myself to consume the next podcast in the queue. My Instagram filled up with inspirational quotes, my email overflowed with ten-step methods for hearing from God and finding your purpose. My favorite worship songs on Spotify played on repeat.

I was consuming teachings on the Bible, longing for knowledge about God and our human condition, filling my ears with truth-filled music, and seeking out wise teachers. These were all great choices— but soon I began to feel like an observer on the sidelines, watching carefully and cheering on those who were growing and offering their insights. The words and testimonies about what God is like and how he is at work in people's lives are invaluable and useful in bolstering faith, but they are only intended as a supplement, not as a replacement for living freely and lightly.

My Christian faith and the way I was practicing it was a secondhand, watered-down relationship with God—true and genuine but impersonal. I was hungry for more. I wanted to experience him for myself, to find him on the pages of Scripture and in my imagination and deep in my soul. I longed to know what he wanted to say directly to me. Not through messengers, but face to face. Not just in my monthly meetings with my spiritual director, but daily.

So on an ordinary morning in June, I began the Gospel-reading and journaling plan Marilyn had told me about.

Here's how it works: In a blank notebook (at least 90 pages, lined, unlined, spiral-bound, stitched, whatever you like), create a table of contents with the chapter, date, and room for a title you will give the chapter after reading it. So at the very beginning, you'll have a running list of all the chapters for each of the four Gospels: Matthew, Mark, Luke, and John. This took up four pages in my notebook. On each day of reading, you'll start a new journal page with the chapter and date at the top. Then read and take notes and journal as you

feel led. At the end of the reading and journaling, give the day a title and flip back to the table of contents to add the title and date to the corresponding chapter. The title could be a concept that sticks out from a verse or plotline or a character trait of God or whatever the Lord showed you through his Word that day.

It's tempting to read the Bible like an instruction manual for our lives. Not sure what to do? Randomly open the Bible and hope the verse your finger lands on offers guidance. Not sure who you are? Find a Bible character you relate to and see what lessons you can learn from his or her life. Not sure how to deal with a troubling situation? Pick a Scripture and repeat it over and over again, like a mantra. The trouble with this way of thinking about the Bible is that the focus becomes all about *us*.

This daily way of reading through the life and teachings of Jesus was a different Bible experience for me. It forced me to read the story as a whole, to slow down and pay attention to who Jesus is, not just what he did. The stories in the first four books of the New Testament were not new to me; in fact, because they were so familiar, I chose to read them in a different Bible translation so the fresh phrases would invite me to think and comprehend in new ways.

Imperative to this practice was the simple but often overlooked act of posturing my heart to be receptive, opening my eyes to see and

beloved notebook

my mind to notice. Instead of rushing through and simply checking a morning quiet-time box with a cheery *I did my Bible reading for the day!*, this practice was intentional and transforming. My perspective shifted as I made the effort to be still and quiet, invite the Holy Spirit to engage, and train my soul to listen to truth on the pages before me. My approach to each day's reading became less about what the Scriptures could tell me about *me* and more about what they would say about God as displayed by the life, death, and resurrection of Jesus.

● ● ● ● ●

My efforts to untangle myself from the worries of the world thus far looked a lot like trying to get to know *myself* better. I was leaning in close to the mirror, rubbing the fog away, and examining my past, my choices, my life. I was paying attention to my healthy and unhealthy ways of being. I was telling the truth and admitting my weakness, growing clearer about my own personality, and choosing to do things that made me feel like me. But this new way of reading the Gospels moved me beyond just looking at myself. I stopped focusing on the tangled state of my life and the insecurities and uniqueness of who I am and began to transform and heal my soul by placing my attention on God. I can't quite put my finger on how it happened, but a trust was forming that wasn't there before. As I read about God's character displayed through his Son, Jesus, I saw parts of him that I knew in my head but hadn't yet known deeply in my soul.

In the opening pages of the New Testament is a long list of foreign and hard-to-pronounce names; it's the genealogy of Jesus. I would normally just skim over the names and find the family tree slightly interesting but mostly inconsequential. *What does this have to do with me?* But the Lord was kind on day one to open my eyes to the truth underneath as I sat with the first chapter of Matthew. God's plan is mysterious and unconventional (women were included in the family line! Sinful people were named!) yet so precise (14 generations from Abraham to David; 14 generations from David to Babylon; 14 generations from Babylon to Jesus). Do I believe his ways are perfect, orderly, and good intentioned? I began that first day with the title "God Is Good" because this, more than anything, was what I needed to have confirmed.

In the story of the woman accused of adultery (John 8), Jesus bends down to write in the dirt, telling the riled-up crowd that the one without sin can cast the first stone. The only one in the circle without sin is Jesus, and *he doesn't throw a stone!* He is so merciful, full of compassion, and forgiving. The woman was set free in a way my heart longed for. It seemed only fitting to title that day "Free."

In Matthew 8, a leper wants more than anything to be healed of his disease. It not only makes him sick but also makes him an out-cast: untouchable, unlovable by his culture. He falls at Jesus's feet in worship and says, "Lord, you have the power to heal me…if you really want to" (verse 2). And Jesus's response took my breath away: "Of course I want to heal you—be healed!" Of course he wants to heal us! He is good, he wants the best for us, he is able, and he will do it.

When a storm picks up with violent winds and overtaking waves, Jesus sleeps calmly in the stern of the boat. His disciples shake him awake: "Don't you even care that we are all about to die!" (Mark 4:39). We do the same thing, don't we? We look at the storms in our lives and wonder why God isn't doing anything to stop them. *Surely we will die, and he doesn't even care!* But Jesus does care. He turned to the sea and commanded it to calm down, and he faced his disciples and said to them (and to us), "Why are you so afraid? Haven't you learned to trust yet?" (Mark 4:40) *Gulp.* Jesus has authority and power over all things (even the waves and sea obey him!). He is worthy to be trusted, and even when it doesn't look like he's doing what we think he should do, he is still in control. Why, then, am I still afraid? Haven't I learned to trust yet?

"Jesus Is Stirring Things Up" is the title I assigned to John 5. He heals the lowest, dines with sinners, works on the Sabbath, speaks to Samaritan women, and calls children first, all to bring life and

who is this?
Even the
wind and the waves
obey him!

MARK 4:41 NIV

freedom and healing. We read about an ancient pool where the sick and crippled gathered in hopes of being healed: "An angel of God would periodically descend into the pool to stir the waters and the first one who stepped into the pool after the waters swirled would instantly be healed" (John 5:4). The crippled man Jesus encountered was desperate for healing but hopeless. He never would be able to get to the pool first. *Is this really God's character?* I wondered. *Would he offer healing only to those who were the first to get themselves into a crowded pool?* No, that is not his way. Filled with compassion, Jesus heals the man. He offers healing to all for free. Not by our own effort but by His. He stirs things up, changing the way we see and think and live.

Jesus is trustworthy. He is who he has always said he is. He fulfilled the promises and the ancient prophecies, and he completed the work he was sent to do—to be the final sacrifice to put us in right standing with God.

The woman at the well at one point looks at Jesus and says, "This is all so confusing" (John 4:25), and I like that line. In fact, I used it as my title for that day's reading. Sometimes Jesus's ways confuse me. Sometimes I think he sounds rude or overly mysterious, and I wonder why he does what he does and says what he says. Something was so freeing about admitting my confusion, being honest with my lack of understanding, and confessing that I didn't think he was doing it right.

• ◆ ▸ • ◆

This reading and journaling practice is supposed to take 89 days—one day for each chapter of the four Gospels—but it took me seven months, and I feel totally okay with that. In fact, I didn't want it to end. My time in the Gospels became a way for me to slow down, to pay attention, to speak to God and hear from God, to get to know his character. I found myself in parables and recognized my inability to measure up, and I grew more grateful than ever before for Jesus's incredible, upside-down ways that lead us to live freely and lightly.

As I look back through the journal, I clearly see the messages I needed to hear directly from God. I needed to know more than just the Bible stories that were familiar to me. I needed to get to know the One in those stories. I needed to see that he is good, kind, compassionate, and responsive. I needed to be honest about my shortcomings—including my entanglement with the worries of the world. I needed to spend time with him, quietly and intentionally, and prioritize this practice in my busy life. I needed to remember his promises. I needed to slow down and talk to him and *listen*. Because just as I had hoped, he did have things to say to me. I was no longer just a casual observer.

My questions of identity and value ran deep. I knew in my head who God said I was, but until I could fully trust and depend on him,

I would always dance between belief and doubt. This seven-month practice realigned my eyes, gave me space to question, and resulted in a depth of trust I didn't know was missing.

The same thing he said to our friend doubting Thomas, he says to us: "Don't give in to your doubts any longer, just believe!" (John 20:27). We may not be able to see Jesus in the same way his disciples did, but still, he shows himself through the first four books of the New Testament and the nearness of the Holy Spirit. He proves himself worthy of our unwavering faith.

Do you trust him? Do you know that he is good, that he wants to heal you, that he is compassionate, powerful, and loving? Even with all your mistakes fully exposed to him, he doesn't throw a stone. He invites you to come to him through his Word, to get to know him and to discover his unforced rhythms of grace written on the pages of the Gospels. And as you notice and trust in his character, your heart will reset and be filled with gratitude, love, and unfathomable peace.

heart-shaped stone

little black dress

№ 14

INTO THE LIGHT

Years ago, when a stage version of *The Lion King* came to town, Ryan and I dressed up in our finest theater attire and met up with friends for a night out. Our velvet-cushioned seats at Seattle's Paramount Theater were in the front row of the balcony, which made for an optimal view but a touch of fear. One faulty move and you're tumbling over the edge and onto the unsuspecting theatergoers down below. As with all things Broadway and Disney, *The Lion King* was breathtaking. The costumes were elaborate, the sets so lifelike. I don't know how they did it, but I soon stopped noticing that the actors were humans and began to believe they were lions and giraffes and warthogs.

One climactic scene had me forcibly holding myself in my seat, partially for fear I would fall over the edge but also because I didn't want to embarrass Ryan or our friends with a disruptive *Amen!* in the middle of the dark theater. But goodness, if my heart could have just shouted and my body stood in utter worship, I would have.

You may be familiar with the story line of this contemporary classic, but if not, here's my quick synopsis: A lion family rules the pride lands, and the king's jealous brother wants the throne. Simba, the young, precarious future lion king, finds himself in harm's way when he disobeys his father and is lured into danger by his uncle. When his father, King Mufasa, comes to his rescue, Simba is spared, and the king dies at the hands of his brother, Scar, who all the while blames the young cub for his father's death.

Simba, next in line to take the throne, runs away from his home, believing he is at fault for killing his father. His evil uncle Scar takes over as king and is doing a terrible job running the kingdom (to put it mildly). Simba is needed in the pride lands to bring back order and take his place as the lion king, but he doesn't feel worthy. *Who am I?* he questions. *Am I the rightful king? Or the murderous son?* And as in all good musicals, the answer is found through song.

Beneath the light of the moon and star-speckled sky, Simba peers into the watering hole at his reflection. Not only are the questioning eyes and the adolescent mane reflected back to him; but he is also faced with the shame of his past, the fear that maybe he isn't enough, the worry that it's best to stay hidden, living a simple grub-eating life while ignoring his true identity. But he's unsettled and can't keep pushing away the questions and doubts, so he looks more deeply into his reflection for answers: *Who am I?*

And then, with a gentle breeze upon the water, his reflected image blurs and comes back into focus to reveal his father's face, full of wisdom and power and grace. "He lives in you!" booms Rafiki, the sage and slightly terrifying baboon. The choir erupts in song with that compelling African lilt. Simba finally understands the truth—he bears the identity of his father, and despite his imperfections and mistakes and long-carried guilt, his father is with him and in him and well pleased.

I know it is a make-believe scene with a secular song from a Disney play, but it holds such truth. My heart nearly burst as I watched the young lion's disposition completely change. Oh, if we could learn how to look at our own reflection and, like Simba, see our wise, powerful, gracious Father looking back at us with love!

The only way Simba can take on his rightful identity is to look past his reflection—the worries and fears, the titles and failures—and see his father. The same is true for us.

• • • • •

wildflowers

My identity journey was speeding up. I could feel freedom on the horizon, but I was still weepy and tender, the littlest things stirring up memories and questions about my value. On one particularly emotional day, I had an appointment with my spiritual director. I didn't know what God wanted to say to me that day, and my spirit felt a lot like the weather out my window—gloomy. I was sad about my past. Sad that I was still not confident in myself. Sad that I couldn't pull myself together and just get over this emotional and spiritual shakeup. Five years is a long time to deal with the same hard questions, and even though I was finding answers and moving in the direction of healing, I wasn't there yet.

My session with Marilyn went in a new direction. She led me in an exercise to uncover a deeply ingrained belief and ask Jesus to reframe it to release me into embracing my true identity. We prayed together and asked the Holy Spirit to bring up a memory that needed to be healed.

Almost instantly my mind was taken back to a scene I had deliberately tried to forget. It was one of the worst days of summer 20 years earlier, right after my dad unexpectedly left our family. My mom, my younger sister, and I went to the apartment where he was staying to beg him to come home. My once loving, charismatic dad sat numbly staring at us in this dark apartment that looked nothing like home.

The blinds were drawn, the air musty, and the furniture dull, rumpled, and unremarkable. He didn't stand and hug us and cry and say he was sorry and come home with us. He didn't choose us. He just sat there.

"Where was Jesus?" Marilyn asked.

The question surprised me. I had never thought of this before, so I closed my eyes and, in my imagination, saw us back in the scene, this time with Jesus there too. He stood tall behind us with strong but gentle arms around our shoulders. He ushered us out of the darkness of the stale apartment and into the light of the bright summer day. He was sad too. He didn't want our family to fall apart. He didn't want my dad to choose this path.

As I stayed with this scene, I imagined Jesus's words to my broken heart.

Let that go. Don't go back in. You have done all you can do. You have done your job. I am so sad for you and your mom and sisters. This isn't how I wanted it. But he chose this. He is unwell. I still love him, and I will be with him. This burden is no longer yours; it's mine. Let me have this responsibility for your dad's life. It is not your shame to carry. His choices are his own. It will be sad and hard to live without him, but I have so much good planned for you. I have so much life for you, but you have to let this go. You cannot blame yourself for your dad's choices. You were not responsible to bring him back. It is

not your job. It is mine. Trust me with it. It will look
different from what you want, but trust me with it.

It was a reframing of a story I had pushed deep into
my untapped memory, but it had not forgotten me. I'm
the peacekeeper in our family; I take it upon myself to
hold everything together, smooth out disagreements,
solve problems. My dad leaving was not a problem I was
able to resolve. And until that moment, I didn't realize
what a hold it had on me. After my call with Marilyn,
I opened my journal and began to write. I needed to
uncover more, and I couldn't let the moment pass me by.
Here's what came out, as if Jesus was speaking straight
to my heart:

You do not need to work so hard at holding things to-
gether. That's my job. Not yours. I've got this. I always
have. But you're so concerned with the troubles of this
world and this made-up need for approval that you
work and strive and stress and toil and spin. Be free.

I have a purpose and plan for just you. It is good
work just for you that will bring you joy. Put aside

responsibility and worry and this fear that the Emily I created is not enough. Your value is set. No one can add to it or take from it. It does not fluctuate based on what you do or don't do. It doesn't change if you do the right or wrong thing or if anyone sees it. It doesn't change if you disagree or if you disappoint someone. Your value is set. By me. And here's what I say about you: You are chosen. Highly favored. Set free. Fully forgiven. Filled with my goodness. A light.

Release this notion that you need to prove yourself valuable. It traps you. It makes you choose things that are not from me. It hinders your vision and clouds your true identity. Stop doing things because you think it's what will please others—you're trying to avoid disappointing, and that's futile. Be who you are. Make choices that are true to who I made you to be and you will thrive. Otherwise, you are just spinning and feeling dreadful. Unhappy. Always anxious. Motivated by worry, not love.

I paused while writing these healing words and penned this question: *What if the true Emily is a disappointment?*

I knew immediately that this was the most vulnerable fear of my life. *Who am I?* was the first part of the question, but underneath was the root of my insecurity: *Am I enough?* The most horrible narrative and accusations came spewing from within me onto paper:

A chain around your ankle anchors you in that dark, sad room with your dad. It's like a gross, gray figure grasping at you, trying to keep you in there—sadness, shame, failure. He's small and scrappy and ugly but strong. He points a finger of accusation. You didn't do enough. You are not enough. God isn't going to take care of you or anyone you love. You need to do it. Get to work, diligent worker. Do your job. Try harder, do more. It's up to you. Don't let anyone down. There's no room for imperfection. Do it right or don't even try. Everyone is watching you. Don't mess up. If they only knew.

You're all alone. You're not a good friend; look at all the ways you've messed up. You're so selfish. Close up and just stick to yourself. You're not a good mom; you need to do more. You're not an athlete. Your skin is pale. You say dumb things. Just stop talking. Be numb. Roll into a ball. Be sad. Be isolated. What kind of person are you? Your house is a mess. Your car is dirty. Your ring is too small. You'll never succeed. Work harder. She's better than you. Why can't you be more like that? What's wrong with you?

My pencil stopped moving as tears streamed down my face and ugly sobs formed that I could not hold in. I was so surprised by the mean words and insecurities that had poured out of me. The narratives that burrowed themselves down deep had become so familiar I hadn't even noticed them. I didn't know just how tender I was and how tempting it was to believe the accusations.

Inside me was a courtroom erupting with shouting and finger pointing until finally Jesus, the true judge, pounded his gavel, stood authoritatively, and shouted, *Shhh! Silence! Order in the court!*

I moved my pencil forward on the paper again, this time to record the new truths he longed to fill my heart with:

It's time to renew your mind. To step out of that room. To let go of the sadness, responsibility, lack of trust, and worry—the inexhaustible need to earn your value. Stop spinning. Twirl. Be free. Be you. Awaken, my daughter, and go. Walk into the light with me. You can trust me.

This was my Simba moment. This was the moment when I looked at my own reflection and saw everything: the sadness, the shame, my own inability, the lies that had deeply woven their way into my brain. These words played on repeat and kept me frantically trying to prove them untrue.

I saw something else: a kind, present Jesus who didn't look at me that way. He didn't see me the way I saw myself.

Where I saw failure, he saw irreplaceable value.

Where I saw imperfection, he saw forgiveness and generous mercy.

gavel

Where I saw all the ways I was letting everyone down, he saw the promise of a future of joy and peace and love.

Where I felt no option except to sit in a dark room and strive to solve my troubles, he ushered me into the glorious light that offered freedom.

All our inadequacies are covered by the grace of God through his Son, Jesus, so when he looks at us, he sees a beautiful reflection. I don't fully understand it, but I receive it. I pray you do too.

You are a chosen people,
a royal priesthood, a holy nation,
God's special possession,
that you may declare the praises
of him who called you
out of darkness
into his wonderful light.

1 PETER 2:9 NIV

blackberries

№ 15

I THINK I'LL GET A TATTOO

When my group of friends in high school fantasized about what tattoo we would get when we turned 18, my answer was always a dolphin. Not just one dolphin, mind you, but a whole pod of them. On my ankle. Circling like a permanent marine mammal anklet parade. Dolphins are still magical creatures to me, but I'm so glad I do not have them inked onto my skin. This is why they do not let young teenage girls get tattoos. We would make regrettable decisions.

I still don't have a tattoo, but I'm considering it. I think I want the word "abide" scripted in my handwriting in white ink across the inside of my left wrist. I hesitate because it seems like it would really hurt to have a needle poke repetitively on that delicate plot of skin. The point, though, is that it would be a regularly visible reminder, and I need a lot of reminding when it comes to abiding—

that steady, constant *being* with Jesus that's hard for my doing-focused self to grasp.

• • • • •

For my friend Erica's fortieth birthday, she invited a few girlfriends to her aunt and uncle's ranch outside of Santa Barbara, California. She told us we would be staying in the barn on the property, which was all well and fine. And then we showed up, and it turns out that "barn" was code for the most beautifully decorated barn-turned-guesthouse any of us had ever seen.

cowboy hat

The down-filled couches were layered with woven pillows and chunky knit throws. A tasteful collection of cowboy hats hung casually on one wall and oil paintings by her aunt on the others. The ceilings were high, with rustic chandeliers and massive wooden beams. The big picture windows looked out onto the family's vineyards, with rolling hills of all different shades of greens and the orderly stripes of grapevines that stretched far into the distance. It was magnificent. We rode on horseback through the hills, visited the charming shops in town, ate at local farm-to-table restaurants, and stayed up late into the night snacking on fancy things like Marcona almonds and fresh honeycomb.

On one outing, Uncle Larry took us on a tour of the small vineyard. He started growing grapes when the central coast of California was just becoming home to a booming winery industry, and he had a wealth of information to share. We walked a while, and he stopped at one row to tell us about the different varieties of grapes and then moved to another to explain grafting and pruning and the well-timed art of harvesting.

It was a grown-up field trip. We tromped through the vineyard, stood amazed in the warehouse at the endless stacks of barrels of aging wine, popped our heads into the bottling facility, and gathered around the circular table in their tasting room, where we sipped from tiny glasses of white and red, each paired perfectly with a petite cupcake.

I learned more about wine and grapes and farming in that one afternoon than ever before. And it gave me a better understanding of what Jesus was talking about in the vine and branch story I had read countless times in John 15: "I am the vine, you are the branches; he who abides in Me and I in him, he bears much fruit, for apart from Me you can do nothing" (verse 5 NASB).

A branch's purpose is to produce fruit, and it cannot do so without being firmly connected to the vine. The relationship between a branch and the vine is the most important part. They have a belonging and dependency, a beautiful two-way interaction—the branch abides, the vine provides. No amount of trying, working, hustling, dreaming, waiting, or willing can get that branch to make fruit on its own. It must remain on the vine. The vine is the source of all nourishment, support, strength, and life, and it willingly gives. As long as the branch is attached, the vine can provide all it needs to accomplish the good work of growing grapes.

• • • • •

The rhythms of grace that Jesus invites us into will produce in us good, lasting, spiritual fruit. Walking with him, working with him

vineyard

and adopting those rhythms result in lives marked by kindness, patience, and love. These beautiful gifts do not come through our individual efforts. We can try to make all the right choices on our own, try to forgive and be generous and love everyone. We can try to be on our best behavior and work our hardest to create ideal, conflict-free lives, but at some point, we will once again grow weary. Our energy, willpower, enthusiasm, and conviction will eventually run out if we are not connected to an abundant, never-ending source of nourishment. The true answer to how to live in alignment with our purpose and in step with Jesus is that word I want permanently marked on my wrist: *abide.*

The word "abide" is a bit old fashioned; it's not one we use in daily conversation anymore. But it has a rich meaning that is important as we walk with Jesus and learn his unforced ways. Merriam-Webster defines "abide" like this: "To remain stable, to continue in a place, to conform to." Other sources use words such as "await," "remain," "dwell," "continue," or "endure."

What does it look like to abide? How do we reorient our minds and hearts away from our self-interests and our propensity to try to prove our value and toward the one source that will sustain us? I wish Jesus would just lay it all out for us with a three-step process to ensure a life of peace and joy and rest. Instead, he simply says, "Abide in me."

I'm wired to *do*; Jesus asks us to *be*. He promises that as we stay connected to him, he will nourish our souls, he will give life that sustains us, he will cause the good fruit of love, joy, peace, patience, kindness, goodness, faithfulness, gentleness, and self-control (Galatians 5:22-23 NIV) to come through us. *Abiding* means turning our eyes, hearts, and minds to God's goodness, beauty, and truth and keeping them focused *steadfastly* there. Loyally, faithfully committed, and unwavering.

This is why I need the word "abide" written where I will see it daily. I need a permanent reminder that even my very best efforts, my most eloquent mission statement, and my sheer dedication to my purpose will not be enough for a deep, soul-fulfilling, fruit-producing life of love. I can do nothing of spiritual value without him. The ability to walk with Jesus, work with him, and learn his rhythms hinges on dwelling, conforming to, remaining, *abiding* with Jesus, the true vine.

We are all invited into this life-giving, rest-sustaining relationship. Are you a doer, like me? Is it hard for you to remember that it's not all up to you? Take a deep breath, open up those hands once again, and remind yourself of this truth: "You will keep in perfect peace those whose minds are steadfast, because they trust in you" (Isaiah 26:3 NIV).

olive topiary

You will keep
in perfect peace,
all whose minds are steadfast,
because they trust in you.

ISAIAH 26:3 NIV

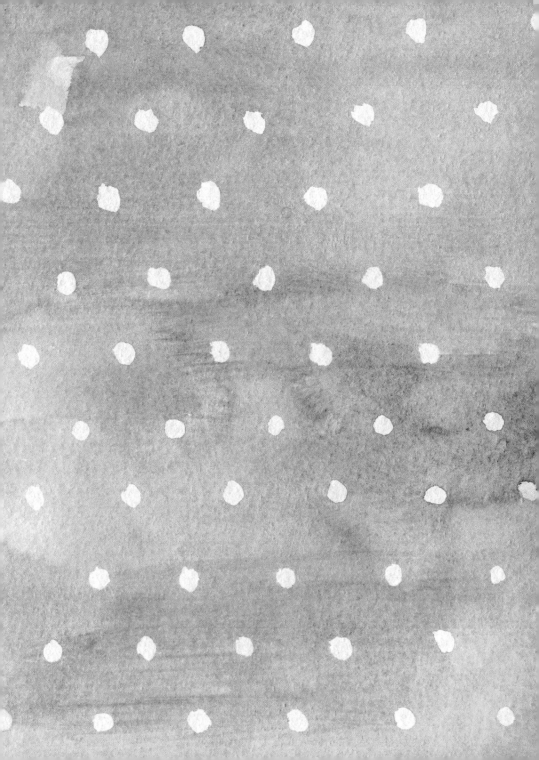

PART FOUR

WE'RE INVITED
TO LIVE FREELY AND LIGHTLY

butterfly

No. 16

FINALLY TWIRLING

I was 25 and newly pregnant. The book *Wild at Heart* by John El-
dredge fell into my hands, and I quickly soaked it up. I was feeling
inadequately prepared for raising the baby boy growing inside me. I
am the middle of three girls with mostly girl cousins and a personal
propensity for all things girly. I was freshly married to my first and
only serious boyfriend and quite unschooled on all things masculine.
This book on manhood was enlightening and encouraging for this
future mom to a son.

Ten months after our baby boy was born and number two was on
the way (I know, so soon!), I picked up the companion to that first
book: *Captivating*, written by the author and his wife, Stasi. I was
sure this next baby would a daughter, and I wanted to savor the wonder of girls. I smiled as I read the chapter about how naturally little

girls seek out the chance to wear dresses that twirl as they spin and dance, hoping to hear confirmation of their loveliness.

Well, I soon forgot about that image and that book *and* about raising a daughter because along came our son Brady. Two years later, we welcomed Mason. My world was not filled with pale pink and delicate dresses as I had expected but with Nerf swords, Lightning McQueen, never-ending wrestling, and potty talk.

It was surprisingly wonderful.

On Thursday mornings, I loaded up the boys, and we headed to church. I dropped them off in their classrooms and took a seat in the main sanctuary for our ladies' Bible study. I looked forward to this weekly reprieve, where the boys played happily and I got a break from toddlers to learn and connect with other women. As the lights dimmed and the hum of conversation quieted, the worship team's voices and the musical instruments filled the room with their offering. I closed my eyes and took a slow, deep breath. It takes effort for me to posture myself fully in the moment, to shake off the worries and to-dos that occupy so much space, and to invite the Holy Spirit to move and make his presence known. Shutting my eyes and focusing on my breath help me find my way to that place.

On one such Thursday, as I sat with mind clear and heart open, the most unexpected picture danced across the dark backdrop of my eyelids. I saw a little girl in an open, grassy meadow with the sun shining down on her. She wore a white ruffled summer dress and twirled with her dainty arms outstretched and her face tilted to the sky. Round and round she turned on tippy-toes, the sweetest smile on her face, her loose hair trailing down her back. So light, so free. I watched her spin across my imagination and felt these words in my soul: *Emily, I am so pleased with who you are. And now, just like that little girl, I want you to twirl.*

It was a lovely vision and a peace-filled message, but it struck me as strange. *God, you're asking me to twirl? What does that even mean?* A quick flash of memory brought back a scene from that womanhood book I read a few years before, and I knew.

From the earliest age, women long to feel seen, important, and beautiful. A little girl adorned with plastic costume jewelry and a sparkly tiara will climb atop the coffee table and spin around until the skirt of her dress swirls around her, all the while gleefully shouting, "Daddy, Daddy, look at me!" She will dance without a care as her father looks on her adoringly. She feels no self-consciousness, and her father offers no criticism of her twirling ability. That Thursday morning, in the middle of Bible study, I remembered that part in the book and knew God was using it to tell me something important.

DRESS-UP THINGS

tiara

wand

necklace

tutu

Another year came and went. I stood again in that same church sanctuary, with a rubber band securing the button of my too-snug jeans and my skin glowing once again with pregnancy hormones, and this time the word "DELIGHT" flashed in all caps across my closed eyelids. I knew the baby I carried was a girl, and I had been praying for a special Bible verse for her, like the one we had for her three big brothers. I flipped my leather-bound Bible to the very back, searching for where the word "delight" can be found in Scripture, and I came to Zephaniah 3:17: "The LORD your God is with you. He is mighty to save. He will take great delight in you, He will quiet you with his love, He will rejoice over you with singing" (NIV).

A knowing smile fell across my face. This was for my baby girl, but it was for me too. In my mind, I still carried the vision of the twirling girl in the white dress, believing she was who I was meant to be, but this verse brought even greater clarity. *Well, no wonder God wants me to twirl*, I thought. *It's because he is the one doing the singing!* The most perfect of all fathers says to us, *Stop. Be still. I am with you. I am mighty. Let me quiet you with my love. Will you listen to my voice as I sing my songs of delight over you? You are just as I want you to be. Now, be free and twirl.*

I knew these words were true. I knew God loved me. I knew he chose me. I knew I could do nothing to earn his grace. I knew that unlike my own dad, he was a father who didn't leave. I *knew* all of this.

This sweet picture was a promise God laid before me, telling me who I am and how I am to live, and it's an image I held protectively in my heart for *years*.

"Twirl" became the motto of my thirties. I had it stamped on wood pencils, I wore a necklace with the word engraved on it, I hung an art print in Audrey's nursery with it lettered in the most perfect, swirly, gold-foiled script. But even then, I didn't quite grasp how to live it, and this incongruency frustrated me to no end. How could I have heard his full message and still not *get* it?

For nearly a decade, I returned to that image of the little girl twirling, and I longed to be her. I was twirling, all right, but I felt far from light and free. In my best effort, I adorned myself in skinny jeans and a tee, climbed atop a platform as if it were a stage and spun around, shouting in my own subtle and not-so-subtle ways, "Look at me! Look at me!" My eyes scanned the imaginary crowd as I wondered, *Who is watching? Who is noticing? Please, somebody, tell me who I am! Tell me I am lovely and wonderful and good at twirling!* Sometimes the audience cheered loudly with approval, and other times, they were a touch critical or, even worse, silent. That just motivated me to twirl harder, faster, until finally, I wobbled to the ground, so tired and burdened and exhausted from a lifetime of trying to earn my value. Thankfully, the Lord didn't let me stay in that dizzy heap. He gently pulled me up, offering rest and a new way to live, and I accepted his invitation.

• • • • •

Here is our final invitation from Jesus: "Keep company with me and you'll learn to live freely and lightly" (Matthew 11:28-30 MSG). Goodness, it's the most beautiful promise, isn't it? Yes, I'll gladly trade burdened and heavy for free and light! When we live in connection to Jesus, we gain a secure, restful, free, and light inner disposition. We practice self-acceptance and are faithful to our path and purpose. We are authentic and obedient. We are present, forgiving, and contented. We show kindness and live generously as our true selves.

Jesus's invitations to recover our lives, take a real rest, learn the unforced rhythms of grace, and then live freely and lightly are all wonderful and worthy of our attention. But what matters most is that our lives are changed, our hearts are set free, and our self-dependence is replaced with a trust in God. This is a transformation of the heart. It is not always easy to see with our eyes, but as we continue to walk with him, work with him, keep company with him, we can't help but be changed.

• ◆ ▸ • ◆

My mind, heart, and spirit have been transforming since that day on the Hawaiian beach when I tearfully whispered the question that fueled this identity journey: *Who am I?* My heart felt lighter. I was no longer tangled up, frantically treading water in my soul, or clouded in my vision of my true identity. It was a long, deliberate, slow journey to become myself.

Five years later, I was once again in Hawaii: this time to celebrate my fortieth birthday. I hoped for a full-circle moment on the beach where I would finally receive the answer. And it *did* happen—just not in the perfect way I had envisioned.

One late afternoon, Ryan and I found ourselves in a disagreement (it happens in normal life and on vacation—ugh!). We each needed a moment to think and be alone, so I made my way down to the white sand beach to watch the waves and talk with Jesus. My old friend Insecurity made herself comfortable next to me on the sand and began to shape my thoughts: *What if being the real me lets people down? What if who I am is not enough?* As I sat looking out on the sparkling turquoise ocean, the true answer to the question washed over me.

beach chair

God wants me to be me. He is not disappointed. He is a delighted, proud Father who desires nothing more than for me to find his opinion of me more important than anyone else's. When I know who I am and then walk quietly and confidently in that knowledge, it brings him glory.

I pulled out my phone and began to write a list—*the* list I had been waiting to write for so long. It was the answer to the question that kept me searching and brought me healing and freedom:

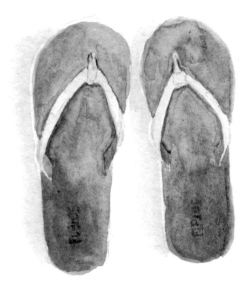

flip flops

Who am I?

I am valuable.

I am chosen.

I am forgiven.

I am made whole, full of peace.

I am creative.

I am curious.

I am happier in the shade than the sun.

I am happier in layers than a swimsuit.

I am happier drinking water than anything else.

I am good with kids.

I am a loving, caring mom.

I am stylish.

I am strong.

I am graceful.

I am elegant.

I am quiet.

I am funny.

I love Jesus and his ways and Word.

I am sensitive to the Holy Spirit.

I am a good listener and question asker.

I am good at baking and homemaking.

I am smart.

I am a good writer.

I am sensitive.

I am empathetic.

I am an artist.

I am okay. Just as I am.

See that last line? That's the one that truly matters. When you decide to be yourself, you might let people down. It's true. At some point, you will disappoint or make a mistake or not be everyone's favorite person. But I am okay, just as I am. You are okay, just as you are. Not because we are wonderful on our own but because God chose us, formed us, dwells in us, delights in us, and calls us *his* own. We are enough because when he looks at us, he sees a reflection of his own beauty, goodness, and truth.

It finally made sense: That's what twirling is all about. Twirling is the natural response when you believe and live in the confidence of his unfailing love, unconditional acceptance, and unwavering nearness. It's remembering that you have nothing left to do or prove. Twirling is the undeniable desire and willingness to stretch out your arms, tip your head back, and move through your beautiful, messy, imperfect, layered life with freedom and grace. It is what happens when your soul is at rest. This is what it means to live freely and lightly. After all this time, I was finally twirling.

The Lord your God is with you,
He is mighty to save
He will take great delight in you,
He will quiet you with his love
He will rejoice over you with singing

ZEPHANIAH 3:17 NIV

telephone

№ 17

MAKE GOOD CHOICES

My phone pinged with a new text message. It was from my Pilates and barre studio: "Lianne asked me to contact you to see if you are interested in going through the barre certification program. We're hosting a weekend program and checking to see who might be joining us."

To most, this would just be an informational text. *You take barre. We're offering a certification program. Are you interested?* But to me, it felt like so much more.

Barre is my favorite workout. I waited way too long into my adulthood to adopt a healthy habit of regularly working out my body, but since joining the studio on my thirty-ninth birthday, I've been sticking to it ever since.

Lianne, the owner of the studio, is a fitness teacher extraordinaire, a former dancer, and the toughest of all the instructors. When she has been on vacation or missed one of her own workouts, she's particularly punishing to the class, in the best way possible (although my abs the next day do not agree). Being asked to join a barre-training program with her was the highest compliment. I felt chosen; I was seen as competent, as showing real potential and promise.

Whether it was truly a vote of confidence in my barre ability or not, it did feel good to be selected, invited, included. However, one of the transformational things I've learned is that those feelings don't get to tell me what to do.

It didn't take much imagination to envision what could unfold if I said yes to the next step. Near-future Emily would get excited. She would think to herself, *Someone—a person of authority—thinks I'm valuable and invited me to do this thing she thinks I would be good at. I should do it!* She signs up, goes through the program, enjoys it, starts teaching classes. Maybe she ends up loving this new thing, or maybe she grows to resent it. She finds herself heading to another class and thinks, *Remember when I did barre because I loved how it felt? How it was a quiet time for me to connect with my body and push myself? How it was one of the first things I did not for accolades or to be seen but to use and appreciate the body God gave me and to move in a way that felt like worship and brought peace and joy? I miss those days.*

This has been an ongoing cycle in my life. Traditionally, I care a lot about what others think of me, which means I am crushed when I'm left out or overlooked, and I spring to life when someone shows an ounce of interest. Because I'm not naturally super-passionate on my own, if someone offers a suggestion or presents me with an idea about what I should (or could) do, I nonchalantly shrug my shoulders and think, *Sure, why not?*

A person says, "We're all in choir. You should join choir!" So I do, but I'm not a very good singer, and I spend an entire year wearing an itchy, floor-length satin gown in church sanctuaries lip-syncing next to the genuinely talented singers.

Someone suggests, "We're all going running. You should come with us!" So I do even though I know I don't like running and feel like my lungs are about to burst and can't keep up and don't have the stamina to run and carry on a conversation, so it's not even enjoyable.

A friend tells me, "You have great style. You should pitch a design show!" So I do, and I work with a production team to create a sizzle reel and wait patiently to hear from the networks and ultimately realize that this

silverware

thing someone suggested I do was never mine to do in the first place.

The examples could go on and on. Getting a haircut that is not right for your hair. Buying the jeans your friend says look great on you but feeling uncomfortable in them. Choosing a job or college or major because it's what your parents want for you.

Do you do this to yourself? Do you try on personalities and jobs and literal outfits that are not yours to wear? When we live from a place of people pleasing, trying to fit in, and wanting the success of others, we end up dressed up as someone else. But is that really what's best for us? Costumes are fun for special occasions, but not for every day.

• • • • •

When my sisters and I were little, our family would pull up to a restaurant or church or a family gathering in our brown Volkswagen Vanagon, and my dad would inevitably turn in his driver's seat to face us and say, "Girls, be on your best behavior!" We would smile at the routine command and then roll our eyes and oblige him. Our parents raised us to have manners and be courteous, and we were often complimented for our behavior.

When I had kids of my own, I chose a slightly different phrase to encourage fine manners and solicit eye rolls from my children: "Make good choices." It's like *Be on your best behavior*, but one notch deeper.

Yes, I want the kids to keep their elbows off the table and say please and thank-you, but even more than having a firm handshake and making eye contact, I want them to pay attention to what matters and realize their choices have an impact.

Being on our best behavior sets us up for trying to win the approval of others through surface-level actions. Making good choices helps us focus on deciding not only *what* to do but *who* we want to become. What type of person do you want to be, and which choice best lines up with that? We make a million small decisions and have the responsibility and agency to decide what path to take. More than anything, making good choices awakens us to who God made us to be, who he is forming us into, and which purposes he has set before us. This is the life skill I want to pass down to my children.

Yes, I could become a barre instructor. But when I look at my life and see what God is doing, where he is leading me, and what I already have in front of me, I can't shrug my shoulders, say yes simply because I was asked, and assume it's the right choice. We must honor our personalities, pay attention to our preferences, understand our motivations, listen to the promptings of the Holy Spirit, and stay aware of the work God has placed before us and remain faithful to that end. This is what makes a good choice.

ribbon

scotch tape

glue gun

glitter

sussors

If any of you lacks wisdom,
you should ask God,
who gives generously
to all
without finding fault,
and it will be given to you.

JAMES 1:5 NIV

Our church announced they were starting a Mothers of Preschoolers (MOPs) group and were looking for help with childcare. My heart skipped in my chest. When the boys were little, I joined a MOPs group and was so grateful for the sweet ladies who took care of the kids while the other moms enjoyed an encouraging morning with food prepared for us, a speaker to inspire us, and a craft time that sparked conversation. I knew volunteering to watch toddlers once a month to give mothers a needed break and time of fellowship was a very good choice and my next right step. My friend Erica signed up too.

A week before MOPs began, Erica was asked to be a table leader for the moms instead of a childcare worker. It was a better spot for her, honestly, as she wasn't super-excited about hanging out with toddlers and is much better suited for developing friendships and offering en-couragement to young moms. Even so, I felt a little ping of jealousy when I found out. Why was she asked to do the more important job and I wasn't? And then, of course, I remembered: Helping in the toddler room was a good choice for *me*. It was a choice I made not for recognition but out of obedience and authenticity. I *adore* kids, and this was a way for me to serve out of my very best gifts. Our greatest joy is to live and make choices that are in line with who God made us to be and what he is asking us to do.

Each Tuesday morning when it was a MOPs day, I came home

beaming. Being with those sweet toddlers filled me up. And Erica made an impact on the women around her table. We each had a place where our best gifts were put to use.

I'm so tempted to compare. It's easy to get caught up in what I think I should do or be or act like or wear. Like a little kid who grabs a cookie without thinking, my natural inclination is to move impulsively toward all manner of good things. But not all good things are mine to do. It takes effort to make wise, deliberate, authentic, and obedient choices not based on my interpretation of circumstances but through the lens of a Father who is trustworthy and completely in charge. *This* is what leads to a free and light life.

We are invited to live freely and lightly as we remain connected to Jesus and allow him to inform our choices. You and I were perfectly and wonderfully made, and we will find peace and great joy when we stay in step with who God made us to be and who we are becoming.

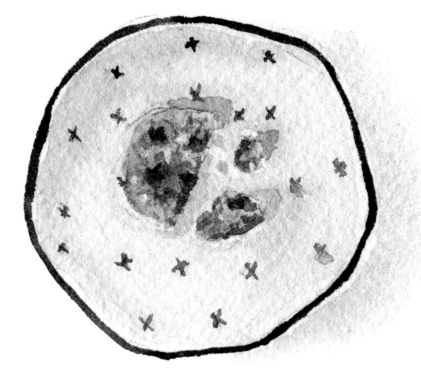

chocolate chip cookies

bag

$\mathcal{N}^{\underline{o.}}$ 18

WEAR IT WELL

Pregnant women have strange cravings. There's the common but completely odd combination of pickles and ice cream. My friend K.C. just wanted cheeseburgers, and my friend Jessica went through bags and bags of gummy bears. When I was pregnant with all four babies, I craved ice. Crushed, cubed, those tiny pellets you get at Taco Time—it didn't matter. In the Starbucks drive-through, Ryan ordered his grande drip coffee, and all I ever wanted was a grande cup of ice. Seriously, it was like dessert to me. This was great for its calorie count but not so great as far as health goes; it was an indication that my iron levels were very low. I took iron supplements and delivered healthy babies, but still, the ice craving continued.

Chewing ice did nothing to improve my iron levels. I knew this, of course. My body was trying to tell me it was unwell, but instead of actually looking to the root of the problem, I kept filling my cup with ice and crunching away to satisfy the craving.

When I decided it was time to listen to my body, I went to a naturopath for supplements to regulate my iron. As my body healed, my ice craving began to wane. It was a great sign, the best sign! And one day, I realized the craving was gone completely. I still enjoyed ice, but I no longer *needed* it to quell the impulse that had become a distraction from real healing.

Soon I had the occasion to notice that ice wasn't the only thing I'd been using as a distraction from my root problems.

• ◆ ▶ • ◀

At the end of each month, I wrote a wrap-up blog post with a few things I had learned, what I had read and listened to, and what I had bought. That particular month, that last category made me wince. *I bought too much.* I had reasons—good reasons—for many of the purchases, so not everything was a waste. But as I wrote my list of all the fun purchases I had made over the month, I had a bit of a gut check.

I bought too much because it felt good to have new things.

I bought too much because of the thrill of the UPS truck delivering a package.

I bought too much because I saw what other people had, and I wanted those cute things.

I bought too much because I have a bad habit of buying too much.

These realizations made me pause. I didn't want to be like this, and I hadn't noticed before how I was distracting myself with the satisfaction of purchases instead of paying attention to healthy living. I knew life with Jesus did not include filling my online shopping cart with more stuff to get a quick boost of superficial serotonin. So I listened to the still, small voice questioning this way of being and decided to make a change.

I started by challenging myself to buy only necessary things for one month. I didn't tell anyone about it and didn't want to make a big deal out of it. It was a way to walk with Jesus in the free and light way he promises. When I wanted a shirt that looked super cute on a girl I followed on Instagram, I stopped myself. When the thing I had my eye on went on sale, when I ran out of the product, when it just sounded fun to switch out the couch pillows, I forced myself to pause the impulse to purchase and paid close attention to my feelings.

Did I need this? Did my kids need this? Was it just more stuff? And most importantly, what longing was I trying to fill? Was my desire to buy about the shirt / lip gloss / decor item, or was it about something else?

Amazon boxes

What started as a one-month challenge went on for multiple months. And the craziest thing happened: As I stopped buying, I stopped wanting. By waking up to the ways I use consumerism to try to heal insecurity, anxiety, boredom, and comparison, the "buy now" button gradually lost its power over me.

Don't be fooled. I like a new sweater as much as the next person, and I find pleasure in pretty clothes and home accessories. In fact, I just ordered a new top to wear to an event, and I'll have great fun opening the package when it arrives. But what I understand now is that just as chewing ice was doing nothing for my iron levels, buying more stuff will do nothing for an off-kilter sense of self. The itch to feel accepted, admired, and appreciated was never fully satisfied by the habits I created to scratch it.

This conscious purchasing shifted my perspective in other areas too. I began to wear less makeup. I know that sounds weird, but for me, it was a big deal. If I could only wear one beauty product for the rest of my life, it would always and forever be mascara. My lashes are long but light, and I have always felt like I look either 12 years old or rather sickly without a swipe of mascara. I wore lash extensions for years and was rarely seen outside *or* inside the house without a heavy coat of L'Oréal Voluminous mascara in black-brown. Maybe getting older helped me relax a little on the self-consciousness, but I think it

mascara

was more than that: I was feeling more comfortable in my own skin.

Speaking of skin, that was another area of newfound insight and acceptance.

●　◆　▪　●　◆

At some point in my early years, I realized with a bit of dismay that my skin was different. Everyone else could lay out and get tan, but I only grew uncomfortably pink and more freckled. I appreciated my red hair, but I didn't like the fair complexion that went with it. Somewhere along the line, I grabbed hold of the belief that my pale skin was bad, that it was ugly and something to fix. I covered it up. I slathered on self-tanner. I baked in a tanning bed. I endured the heat to try to get just a little bit of color. I made sure I was first to make a pale-skin joke while among perfectly golden-skinned friends, and I've said a thousand times how thankful I am the kids got their daddy's darker skin, not mine. For as long as I can remember, my internal mean girl shamed me for the skin I was in.

So imagine my surprise the day Ryan shouted from across the parking lot, "I like your freckles!" and I called back, "I like them too!"

Emily from even a year prior would have smiled and then made a self-deprecating comment. Instead, my instinct was to stand in agreement. I realized then that I was growing. Not only did I no longer despise my skin, but I had come to accept it. And even better, I was beginning to find beauty in the way God made me.

● ◆ ■ ● ◆

When I began to work out regularly, I didn't see lower numbers on the scale. If anything, my weight went up a few pounds (muscle, I hoped). I *felt* stronger. I could make it through the full barre workout without needing to give my glutes or quads a break. I moved up to three-pound weights. I climbed stairs with more pep and beat my teenage boys at a planking contest. My body didn't completely change, and I'm not sure anyone even noticed, but I saw clear signs of incremental transformation.

So it was with my heart, mind, and soul. We can't step on scales to measure our progress toward increased joy, love, peace, and awareness of God's presence. But when I stopped to notice, the signs of growth were evident. Deeper trust. Quick repentance. Bravely showing up as the authentic me. Kindness toward myself and compassion for others. The once-automatic responses that bound me in a life of insecurity and self-protection began to shift as I kept company with Jesus. I can't explain how it worked, but slowly, my heart aligned with his, my mind took on his way of thinking, and as I become more like him, I become more truly myself.

I wasn't sure if anyone else was noticing the changes in me until the night we gathered for an extended family dinner.

Ryan's grandpa sat across from me. He didn't say much during the meal. His hearing has declined, and even with a hearing aid, he struggles to track multiple conversations around the dining table. But afterward, as we were gathering our coats and piling leftovers into containers to take with us, he came in close.

"Emily, I was watching your face during dinner. You wear contentment well."

Grandpa Lex is a kindhearted man. He loves his family and loves God's Word and always has thoughtful things to say, even if he does say them just a touch closer inside my personal space than I prefer. I thanked him, grabbed my bag, and hugged the family, and we drove home. But his statement stayed with me long after that night. *You wear contentment well.* No one has ever said this to me, and it was an instant encouragement that maybe this new way of following Jesus was working. Perhaps the changes taking place inside my soul were becoming noticeable to the outside world.

• • • • •

We find true, lasting satisfaction when we are content with who we are and with God's plan and purpose for our lives. When we trust him, when we delight in his goodness and promises and care for us, we don't need to look anywhere else to fill the longing to belong. We can stand confidently in our identities as individuals who are securely loved, completely forgiven, and abundantly provided for, whether we're wearing this season's shoes or not, whether our faces are made up or not, whether we have a bustling business or not, or whether we have an overflowing savings account or not.

For so long, my hope was misplaced and my desires were grossly out of order. I was choosing temporary

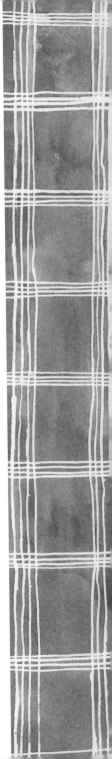

fixes to satiate insecurities that would never be solved with superficial solutions. Jesus rescued me, offering lasting satisfaction, complete fulfillment, peaceful contentment, and grace on top of grace.

Jesus is sufficient to take care of all of our needs, to sustain and restore and breathe new life into us. Adopting his way of living is not always easy, and it does not guarantee that all will be well. And yet somehow, when Jesus comes in and transforms our hearts, on the inside, all is well. He whispers new dreams and puts our souls at ease. He changes our desires and settles us down. He offers hope that goes beyond our circumstances and our ability to control. We still have wants. We still have issues. We still have hopes we long for and difficulties to endure, but the heart posture is different. Where it once craved to be soothed with temporary fixes, it is now fully satisfied by the love and acceptance of a very good Father.

What a delightful surprise when the beautiful healing happening on the inside begins to show itself as settled contentment in our lives and on our faces.

May the God of hope
fill you with all joy and peace
as you trust in him,
so that you may
overflow with hope
by the power of the Holy Spirit.

ROMANS 15:13 NIV

striped shirt

№ 19

GOOD AND TRUE

My bedroom closet is the place I go when I need to be quiet and alone to talk to God. It's tucked away behind our room, through the big bathroom in the back of the house, and no one thinks to look for me there. The hanging clothes, lined-up shoes, baskets of socks, and drying unmentionables give it a muffled coziness. The window lets in a little bit of light and fresh air, and the carpet creates a nice spot to kneel or lie down as I posture myself humbly before God.

I don't always go to my closet to pray. I pray in the shower or car or on the couch or in a coffee shop as I'm journaling. Prayer, I've learned, is an ongoing awareness of God's nearness and the internal dialogue that happens between us all day through. But at times, when I'm especially burdened or desperate, the closet is where I go for a special meeting with God.

That's where I was one morning in late November: on my knees, folded over with my forehead on the ground, asking, *What now?* I had tears in my eyes because I cry easily and was so desperate for an answer. Jesus had set me free, released me from the tangle of weeds I was caught in, and offered peace and contentment and joy in fresh ways.

I was so grateful...and I had no idea what to do next.

I was struggling with how to move forward in a way that honored Jesus and was genuine to me; I needed clear direction. He was so gracious to answer, and he spoke gently to my heart right there among the blouses and dresses and T-shirts: *Be an artist.*

I know hearing God is a weird thing, and not everyone has moments when it is as obvious as this, but when you know it's God, you just know. Just the other night, Brady was telling Ryan and me what the Lord spoke to him at youth group, and Audrey overheard.

Our daughter expressed her uncertainty: "I don't get it. God doesn't say things out loud to me. How do you know when you hear him talk to you?"

Brady's answer was thoughtful and confident: "Words just come into my mind, and I know they are not words I would think. They feel so calming and good and true."

My son's response summed up how I felt that morning on the closet floor. God's answer to my soul question felt calming and good and true. *Be an artist.*

Now, here's the thing: I don't think God is going to ask us to be something that completely shocks us or is incongruent with who we already are. So while I wasn't expecting the response I received, it fit me. It *was* me. I love creating and decorating and painting and making. I always have. If someone were to describe me in one word, they would likely choose "creative." For as long as I can remember, I was drawing, sketching, writing, or dreaming up something. Art has always been a thing I've done. But he didn't say *do* art. He said *be* an artist.

• • • • •

I built a career centered around my creativity. I designed stationery, did graphic design, took pictures, and sold art prints, but never in a million years would I dream of introducing myself as Emily, the artist. That sounded way too fancy for the things I do.

I think of a real artist as someone who makes fine art, went to art school, displays their work in galleries, and enters art competitions and shows. Artists were angsty and maybe a little dark, wore cool clothes, and created things that looked like a bunch of paint speckles but had odd, philosophical titles. My art looked less like curious abstract paintings and more like tissue-paper flowers made during the kids' nap time, cartoony doodles on the back of Starbucks napkins, quotes lettered in my fake calligraphy style, and simple watercolor illustrations. I *did* art, but I would never call myself an artist. And I think that was the problem.

Deep, deep down in the truest part of me, I am an artist. I always have been. But instead of living confidently in that, I've tried to be other things and pushed the artist part way down. I told myself that being an artist was secondary to more important characteristics, like innovation and strategy and growth that mattered in the world of online business I was in. I was trying to focus on what I thought I was supposed to do as an entrepreneur, but honestly, it wasn't clicking. Not only was I not especially good at it, but it was starting to burn me out. I became cynical, tired, uninspired, done. That's the thing: When we are not being who we were made to be, it drains the life right out of us. And that's what led me to that crisp fall morning, crying out to God to please, please, *please* help me figure this thing out.

● ● ◗ ● ◗

Be an artist, he said.

It was so clear and concise, and I had no desire to ignore or dismiss it. If I have learned anything about God, it is that he has good intentions for us. If he offers guidance, it's always in our best interest to listen and obey. I took the directive very literally, and within the next few days, I spread my long-neglected watercolor paints and brushes and pad of thick paper out on the kitchen table and began to paint.

I was working on a painting of a vase of flowers. It was nearly Christmas, so the blossoms had a Christmas-y feel to them, with reds and deep greens and dotted berries in a black-and-white striped vase. I saw a potential for cuteness, but I wasn't sure I was succeeding. I needed to step away. I like to let the paint dry between layers, and while waiting, I ran upstairs. I remember thinking to myself as I climbed the stairs, *That painting is terrible. I'm not an artist. I don't even know what I'm doing.*

How quickly I had forgotten what God said.

Moments later, when I returned, Ryan was standing over the drying painting and exclaimed, "Em, this is amazing! How did you do that?" The contrast was not lost on me.

I could choose to be hard on myself, compare, set unrealistic expectations, ignore the call on my life, and give up, or I could lean into the gifts God gave me, listen to positive voices from people who love

christmas bouquet

and care about me, and keep trying. This whole renewing your mind thing is real, my friend. It requires deliberately paying attention, taking thoughts captive, and deciding whose opinion wins out. Which voice would I listen to? The one telling me I was terrible and should give up or the one saying, "This is who you are. Now be it"?

I continued working on that flower painting and ended up mildly liking it. My older sister Amy, who is my biggest cheerleader, asked for a copy and immediately put it on proud display in her kitchen. Her enthusiasm spurred me on. After the flowers, I moved on to other subjects and liked those even more. *Hmm*, I thought. *Maybe I am okay at this.* For the next week, the watercolors stayed out on the kitchen table, and I played around with them, painting little doodles and patterns, keeping some of them, tossing the rest.

On New Year's Day, I had a moment of inspiration: *What if I used the year to practice being an artist? What if I challenged myself to look at everyday, ordinary things and instead of taking photos of them (as I have done throughout years of regular blogging and Instagram posting), I painted them? What if I did a simple painting every single day for the whole year? What if being an artist takes practice, and this was my opportunity to try?* So on January 1, 2019, I started a yearlong painting challenge. My first piece was of a paperwhite bulb in a favorite geometric-patterned planter sitting on the kitchen counter. I added a shadow to mimic other artists and captioned it "A Paperwhite Waiting to Bloom."

All year, every single day, I painted. I set up a desk in my office to keep all my supplies out, and each afternoon, as I quieted my mind, I chose a subject to sketch and paint. Some paintings told stories about the day—a toothbrush and toothpaste on the day we all had dentist appointments, a bag of cough drops when I wasn't feeling so great, a box of Lucky Charms on St. Patrick's Day, a maple leaf turning colors in early fall. Sometimes I painted things that stirred up a cherished story I wanted to share, like my grandma's antique ring she passed down to me, a bouquet of balloons to illustrate a Scripture I read that morning, a Hawaiian shirt in honor of our dads on Father's Day. I tried my hand at loose landscapes and animals and seasonal flora and fauna and surprised myself nearly every single day with how well the paintings turned out.

Over my year of creating daily paintings, I learned to *be* an artist. I practiced every day, withholding harsh judgment, and trusted I was using my gifts to the best of my ability. The practice certainly helped improve my art—the paintings toward the end of the year are decidedly more detailed and refined than those at the beginning. I am more confident with sketching, mixing colors, and shading than I was before. But the daily discipline became more than just painting cute things. It turned into a daily spiritual practice—a way for me to

WATERCOLOR ESSENTIALS

paint

brush

palette

stand in agreement with what God says of me and be fully myself. I learned to slow down, pay attention, notice, and capture the beauty of regular, ordinary life in lovely watercolors. The year of paintings did more than just make me a better artist. It continued the work of healing my heart, mind, and soul.

Each of us has gifts and talents and passions inside. We do not pursue these to prove our value or give our lives meaning. Instead, out of a deep, abiding trust in God, we use them to become the people he always intended for us to be—quietly confident, contented, and full of unrelenting trust even when life is not as smooth as we wish. And we use these gifts he's given us as an offering back to him. Jesus replaces our once anxious, burdened hearts with hope, joy, and peace, and out of that overflow, we use all variety of gifts for his glory.

● ● ● ● ●

I turned on the radio, and the Christmas carol "Little Drummer Boy" was playing. I'm particularly fond of Justin Bieber's snappy rendition, but this one by For King and Country captured my attention as I drove home on the still-dark roads after dropping Ethan off at school. I listened to the story of the poor boy who hadn't a valuable gift to bring to the new baby King and saw a glimmer of myself in the story. Maybe you identify with him too.

And whatever you do,
whether in word or deed,
do it all in the name
of the Lord Jesus,
giving thanks
to God the Father
through him.

COLOSSIANS 3:17 NIV

Jesus is so worthy of being honored and deserves only the most luxurious of all gifts. Yet there we stand with our wounds, our baggage, our bad habits, and our wavering faith, and still, he asks us to come. He just wants us to show up as ourselves—fully forgiven, completely accepted—and give our lives, our hands, and our hearts back to him as an offering.

So we play the drum. We paint. We fight for the weak. We build and sew and teach. We design lovely spaces and cook magnificent (or not so magnificent) meals. We start businesses, take photographs, write words, tell stories, calculate figures. We do this all because this is what makes us *us*. We don't have to try to do or be what we think is expected of us; we get to be fully ourselves. We use our one-of-a-kind mix of talent, voice, community, career, culture, and time in history to share the good news of who Jesus is and what he has done for us as only we can do. We do this not for recognition or to prove our value but because it is all we have to offer, and we can't help but bring something to the One who gives us life.

My favorite piece of the classic Christmas carol (besides the catchy pa-rum-pum-pum-pum part) comes at the end. "Then, he smiled at me," retells the Drummer Boy. "Me and my drum." Isn't that amazing? A little cheesy, sure, but also true. Jesus is surrounded by precious, valuable gifts, yet he is so pleased with the humble offering of a drum solo.

Whatever our gifts—whether big or small, seemingly important or barely noticed, on display or done in secret—may we offer them generously to a loving Father who receives our offering with a smile. He takes great delight in us being exactly who he made us to be.

Paperwhites waiting to bloom

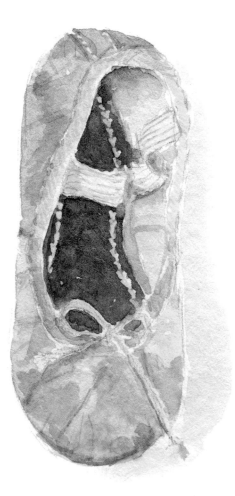

ballet shoe

№ 20

BEAUTIFUL FEET

My first pair of pink ballet slippers are the size of the palm of my hand. In a box on a shelf in Audrey's closet, I keep all my first ballet things: pastel leotards, tiny barely pink tights, a special hand-knit wrap sweater in the prettiest blush hue that Audrey wore to ballet class when she was the same age. Also in that box are the pointe shoes my mom wore as a young dancer. Her old ballet shoes and recital costumes were among my very favorites in our childhood dress-up chest.

My mom grew up in a family of artists. Her father was a brilliant pianist, an actor, and a remarkable painter who worked as a set designer in the 1960s Seattle theater scene. Her mother was a dancer who once taught a dance class to Judy Garland and acted in local theater productions alongside my grandfather. Art of all kinds is a family legacy.

When I was three and a half, my mom signed me up for my first ballet class. That was six months younger than the age preference at Miss Jan Collum's School of Classical Ballet, but because I was a little girl who loved to dance, had an ear for music, and moved gracefully, my mom convinced Miss Jan to make an exception. It was love at first plié.

The large ballet studio with its mirrored walls, large windows, and wooden barres around the perimeter was reserved each week for the instructor, the pianist, and the students. Once a year, folding chairs were set up, and proud moms, dads, and grandparents sat in for a class. Parent Day was indeed a very special day. My mom hired a babysitter for my sisters, and my dad came prepared with a giant camcorder perched on his shoulder to record his toddler ballerina in a home movie.

As Miss Jan introduced herself and gave an overview of our ballet class, the students were instructed to patiently sit on the floor with legs crossed and hands folded gently in their laps. The home movie pans from Miss Jan over to the left, where my dad zooms in on his tiny, redheaded dancer. Instead of sitting properly, my legs are crisscrossed and tucked up to my chest, and I'm spinning around on my bottom with a big grin on my face.

This part of the beloved home movie makes me pause. I've always thought of myself as a rule follower and a people pleaser. My mom says that if ever I was misbehaving, all she had to do was look at me side-ways and I would crumple into a puddle of tears. I don't do well when I disappoint people. Which makes me wonder about this baby version of me. Did she yet know the pressures of seeking approval? Did she feel the eyes of parents and classmates and her ballet mistress on her? Did she know she was expected to always be on her best behavior?

With curiosity and awe, I watch the image of me, who in that moment didn't care about approval. She was living freely and joyfully, too excited to hold still. *This is my place! This is what I'm made to do!* My

ballet sweater

Nutcracker

love for ballet continued through my childhood.

Everything about dancing was life to me: precision, discipline, grace, beauty. I loved taking ballet classes. I loved the teachers. I loved the movement. I loved the classical music. I loved the poking of bobby pins into my hair and the pulling on of smooth tights. I loved feeling graceful, challenging myself with new combinations, using my mind and body so closely together. I even loved auditioning each year because it meant I could be part of *The Nutcracker*, with its bustling backstage, fanciful costumes, makeup, and contagious excitement.

What I didn't love were my feet.

At age 12, I was training with the reputable Pacific Northwest Ballet. It was time to advance to the next level, so the school administrators called my parents in for a meeting. What they communicated was not at all what we had planned for.

"Emily is a very fine dancer. She has the right body. Her neck is long, and her movement is graceful. But she doesn't have the right feet. For her to begin dancing en pointe, she will need more flexibility and a better point. We recommend that she meet with our podiatrist to have the bones of her feet reconstructed if she wants to continue dancing on scholarship at our school."

It didn't take long for my parents to make their decision: No way would they put their 12-year-old through the risk of surgically altering her feet.

And just like that, my ballerina dreams were over. All because of my stupid, messed-up feet.

• ◆ • • ◆

The morning before I turned 40, I sat out on the lanai of our hotel room, watching the sun come up. My phone chimed, and I read this message from my sweet friend:

> *The Lord woke me at four this morning with the most beautiful image of you draped over yourself, drenched in peace and tying up the loveliest, brand-new, dusty-pink toe shoes. And these words, "How beautiful are the feet of those who bring good news." I pray that you might know those feet of yours with new purpose and twirl!*

It feels exceedingly special to pop up in someone's mind in such a clear and Holy Spirit–influenced way. Yet my first response to the picture in her mind and the words Jesus spoke through her about beautiful feet was the faithless thought, *But my feet are not right.*

And then, just as quickly as that lie arose, the truth God wanted me to know and believe flooded over me: *Your feet are just as I made them. They are nothing to be ashamed of, and they have purpose. Good, important, life-giving purpose.*

How beautiful
on the mountains
are the feet
of those who bring good news,
who proclaim peace,
who bring good tidings,
who proclaim salvation,
who say to Zion,
"your God reigns!"

ISAIAH 52:7 NIV

It has taken me a long time and a lot of work to get to this place where the Holy Spirit's voice is louder than my own. As I lifted my gaze from the phone to the glimmering Pacific Ocean before me, I knew this was the turning point.

I could continue believing I was made incorrectly, wishing my feet were different—wishing *I* were different. I could listen to my critical lies and allow them to replay in my mind, nagging at me for the rest of my life, holding me back, and keeping me bound. Or I could trust in God and what *he* says about me and choose a life of complete freedom.

I looked up the Scripture my friend quoted: "How beautiful on the mountains are the feet of those who bring good news, who proclaim peace, who bring good tidings, who proclaim salvation, who say to Zion, 'Your God reigns!'" (Isaiah 52:7 NIV).

I read the word "beautiful" and assume it means "pretty" or "attractive." But have you looked at feet lately? Nope, not beautiful. Scripture isn't saying the feet that bring good news are nice to look at. Instead, here "beautiful" means "befitting, becoming, perfectly appropriate, used as designed."

When the New Testament says something is beautiful, it usually uses the Greek word *horaios*, which means "belonging to the right hour or season; timely; flourishing." It's like a crop that ripens at just the right time or a tool being used for its purpose. I like this definition much better.

Beautiful are the feet that bring good news.

How befitting the one who uses her talent to bring joy to others.

How becoming the one who leaves peace in her wake.

How perfectly appropriate is the one who loves her neighbor.

How timely the one who offers herself to comfort and encourage.

So, yes, my feet are not right for pirouetting on tippy-toes, but the God of the universe calls them perfectly appropriate to be used as designed. He did not make a mistake when he formed my feet without high arches. He didn't mess things up for me by not making my feet ballerina worthy. The feet he gave me are just right for the work he has for me. And your feet are just right for the work he has for you.

As it turns out, this isn't just about our feet. It is about my journey and yours toward becoming exactly who our Creator God made us to be. It is about a God who can use the things about us that we see as weaknesses, as not right and broken, for our own good and his glory.

LEATHER SHOES

boots

sandals

heels

It is about the clear possibility that his plans are better than anything we could come up with on our own. It is about shifting our identities from what we do and say about ourselves to who *he* is and what *he* says about us. It is about living from a place of quiet confidence instead of grasping tirelessly for counterfeit fillers that will never satisfy.

While this transformation takes effort and brutal honesty, woven graciously throughout is a gentle lifting of burdens, a reorientation to truth, and a kindness and compassion that settles us down. We can be ourselves and give ourselves freely and openly, not worrying about doing it right or looking right or having it all together, because our value is set and secured by a God who first loved us.

He's been offering this life of peace and joy from the very beginning, but we have a way of tangling ourselves up in pride and insecurity, falling asleep to the truth, and focusing our eyes on the impossibilities and inadequacies instead of his unending grace and provision. But thank goodness, my friend, that it's never too late. This very moment is befitting, timely, and perfectly appropriate to accept Jesus's generous invitation. So take a deep breath, open up your hands, and may you step freely and lightly into a beautifully abundant life.

our house

EPILOGUE

Our house is a darling cottage with dormer windows and a big front porch on a large stretch of property surrounded by mature evergreen trees. We moved in after returning from our big family road trip around the country, and while we knew we needed a fresh start, we never could have known just how true that was. Leaving the old and familiar is hard, but we were grateful for a new home and community to find belonging in. We once lived side by side with neighbors, packed in tight on tiny postage stamp-sized lots, but now we had room to stretch out, with no need for window coverings or a privacy fence. This sweet, slightly dated but perfectly charming home and its surrounding property felt like a shelter—a quiet, cozy, enveloping embrace.

And then, two years in, we decided it was time to let in some light. Ryan and a friend with a massive tractor cleared the back half of our property. They took down evergreen trees and tore out underbrush. They pushed away scraggly branches and chewed up invasive ground cover. They nearly doubled the size of our backyard and removed the big maple tree that shaded the yard. While it appeared a bit like a hurricane had come through, it also let in so much light. It looked a mess, but there was the promise of progress.

The same clearing and letting in light that happened in our back-yard took place in my heart over the last five years. All the brave and good work of opening up my hands, releasing the beliefs and efforts that tangled me up, and paying attention to the new ways of thinking and seeing had me looking like a bit of a mess and feeling so very tender. It was as though a hurricane had come through, dis-orienting my once comfortable ways, pulling up weeds and thorns, and discarding the ugly remnants of insecurity and lies. But where there was once inky darkness, now there was light. Where there was once self-protective striving, now there was deep trust in a capable God. The heaviness of anxiety in the middle of my chest was released, and I was set free. The freedom and healing had come—and it will come for you too.

• ♦ ▶ ♦ ●

Accepting God's invitation to live freely and lightly is an ongoing, never-ending process. Like our backyard, we don't just take down trees and tear apart the ground and expect that we'll end up with a perfectly landscaped yard. We have to keep working at it.

Do more clearing.

Smooth out the bumps.

Come up with a plan.

Add seed and plants.

Keep it watered and fed.

Watch for weeds and pull them out.

Wait patiently and let the light work its magic to bring new growth.

The transformation of our hearts will cause discomfort. It goes against our self-protective ways and leaves us feeling bare and exposed. But my sweet friend, will you do me the greatest honor? Will you believe me when I tell you it is all for your very best good? God is trustworthy. He is kind and gentle, and he wants your heart to be free and light. Nothing pleases him more than his beloved children accepting his invitation to abundant life.

Every minute of every day, we get to choose. Will we forget who we truly are? Will we look to the world to offer us value, love, and acceptance? Or will we trust that who God is, who he made us to be, and the purposes he has placed in our hearts are where our true

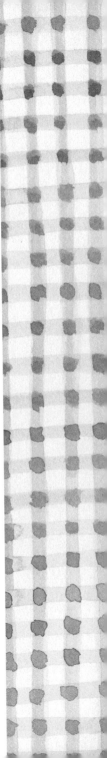

fulfillment rests? Our daily choice to remember, pay attention, and abide—the tiny acts of faith that collect at the end of the day, the week, the month, and the year—adds up to a life of choosing more than just "fine." God invites us to a life of joy, peace, and abundance; it's up to us to accept his gracious invitation. And as we do, his radiant light will work its wonders and cause us to flourish in the most extraordinary, unimaginable ways.

sweet pea

Now to him who is able
to do immeasurably more
than all we ask or imagine,
according to his power
that is at work within us,
to him be the glory in
the church and in
Christ Jesus
throughout all generations,
for ever and ever!

Amen.

EPHESIANS 3:20-21 NIV

THANK-YOUS

On the Monday after returning home from my fortieth birthday trip, I started the day like any other. But as it turned out, this was not an ordinary morning. As I headed down the stairs to start the make breakfast / pack lunches / brush hair / load backpacks routine, I heard a voice in my spirit say so clearly, *It's time to write.*

I stopped midtread, listened, and agreed. *Yes, God. It is time to write.*

I had written a blog for nearly a decade and had journaled regularly, so I easily could have missed the meaning. But in that moment, I knew that the writing he was leading me toward was different. I knew that it was time to write my story of identity and freedom. Jesus had healed me and showed me who I am, and now it was time to write it all down and tell the good news of what he had done in my life. Would it be just for me? Or would I share it publicly? I wasn't sure. I just knew it was time to write.

That morning, after the kids were off to school, I sat down at my desk to begin my workday. At the top of my inbox was a name I was surprised to see. We had spoken months before about book possibilities but ultimately decided it was not the right time. I clicked on the email and read a few lines, and my eyes instantly grew teary. She had taken a new job at a Christian publishing company and was acquiring authors for the next year, and I had come to mind. "Is it time for you to write yet?" she wondered.

And so it began.

Ruth Samsel, I am so thankful for that email. You have been the creative force behind this project and a constant cheerleader. Thank you for believing in me.

Jenni Burke, our story is just as God-ordained. What a delight to have your gentle spirit and literary wisdom in my life.

To the whole team at Harvest House, thank you for making this the very best experience and welcoming me into your publishing family.

To Hope Lyda, my editor and friend. Thank you for the hours and hours of brainstorming, outlining (and re-outlining!), asking questions, praying, encouraging, and digging through my words and stories to find the ones that needed to be shared.

To John Mark Comer, Tim Mackie, and the team at the Bible Project; Alex Seely, Tim Keller, John Piper, and Emily P. Freeman. Unbeknownst to you, your wise voices guided me through this transformation journey. I am greatly influenced by your words, your dedication to your faith, and the ways you encourage others to follow Jesus.

To Joanna, my first best friend.

Jennie Allen, your compassion and grace that night in Rwanda changed the course of my life. Thank you for your bravery in speaking truth.

K.C., Reagan, Jen, and Kelsey, what a treasure it is to have friends to walk with through college, careers, marriage, motherhood, and the process of figuring out who we are. Even though I cry too much during our prayer times, I'm so grateful for them.

Marilyn Vancil, you led me gently through the churning waters to a quiet pool, and I cannot thank you enough. (Note: If you're looking for a biblical take on the Enneagram, please choose Marilyn's book *Self to Lose, Self to Find*).

Emily Jamieson, the Lord made our path cross at all the right moments. The way you listen to the Spirit and allow him to speak through you has changed me. You witnessed the most miraculous healing of my life, and I couldn't ask for a better spiritual sister to share that with.

Erica, you are the friend I didn't know I needed in a time when I really needed a friend. God is so good to give us each other.

To my girlfriends who create space to process, wonder, tear up, question, and be silly and sometimes inappropriate, you make life rich.

To the Jones/Conley/Olason/Isaacson/Owens/Jackson/Yamaka/Lex family, we are an imperfect bunch, but we love each other and are really good at having fun. I'm so glad you're mine.

Amy and Hillary, you are the very best sisters I could ask for.

Mom, you've been through unimaginable heartache, and yet you remain hopeful, inviting, forgiving, and lighthearted. Thank you for all the ways you love us so well.

Ethan, Brady, Mason, and Audrey, the greatest privilege of being your mom is watching you grow into who God uniquely created you to be. I'm delighted by each of you.

Ryan, thank you for choosing a New Year's word that pushed me to reconsider mine. I am forever grateful for your wisdom, your perspective, and your love.

To the longtime readers and supporters of Jones Design Company, what an honor it is to be your online friend. Thank you for sticking with me through the quiet years, and may the years to come be filled with joy and covered in grace as we draw closer to Jesus.

ABOUT THE AUTHOR

Emily Lex delights in catching glimpses of God's goodness, beauty, and truth and encouraging others to do the same. Boxes of journals and a decade of blogging make for thoughtful words and relatable stories—the kind you might enjoy over a cup of coffee with a friend. Her watercolor illustrations bring a charming lightness to all she does. Emily lives with her husband, Ryan, and their four kids in Gig Harbor, Washington, where, yes, it really does rain that much (but you'll never see a prettier summer day).

Visit with Emily at emilylex.com.